DROPOUTS

Second Edition

DROPOUTS

*Who Drops Out and Why—
And the Recommended Action*

By

Robert F. Kronick and Charles H. Hargis

*The University of Tennessee
Knoxville, Tennessee*

CHARLES C THOMAS • PUBLISHER, LTD.
Springfield • Illinois • U.S.A.

Published and Distributed Throughout the World by
CHARLES C THOMAS • PUBLISHER, LTD.
2600 South First Street
Springfield, Illinois 62794-9265

©1998 by CHARLES C THOMAS • PUBLISHER, LTD.
ISBN 0-398-06850-X (paper)

Library of Congress Catalog Card Number: 97-52333

Printed in the United States of America

SM-R-3

Library of Congress Cataloging-in-Publication Data

Kronick, Robert F.
    Dropouts: who drops out and why--and the recommended action /
by Robert F. Kronick and Charles H. Hargis--2nd ed.
        p.   cm.
    Includes bibliographical references (p.) and index
    ISBN 0-398-06850-X (pbk.)
    1. Dropouts--United States. 2. Dropouts--United States--Prevention.
3. Curriculum change--United States. 4. School improvement pro-
grams--United States. 5. Community education--United States.
    I. Hargis, Charles H. II. Title.
LC143.K76 1998
371.2'913' 0973-dc21   97-52333
                                                                      CIP

We would like to dedicate this book to our children, Julia and Will and April and Jill. They have made us appreciate all children. Our wives, Sandra and Linda, have personalized many of the concepts presented in this book.

CONTRIBUTORS

SUZANNE ARP

REBECCA BAKER

CAROL BEILHARZ

CHARLES H. HARGIS

ROBERT F. KRONICK

MARY LEFLER

CAROLYN STINNETT

LINDA THOMAS

LOIDA C. VELAZQUEZ

AMY WOMBLES

PATRICIA YARNELL

PREFACE TO THE FIRST EDITION

The resources for managing the dropout problem are at hand The solution should be of no consequential economic burden. In fact, in implementing the suggested reforms, an immediate salutary effect on both the school and the community should occur.

While these reforms are conservative in the economic sense, they are also conservative in the sense of conservation. We feel that these recom mended reforms will protect and conserve this large segment of our youth for more constructive and contributive lives.

Our appreciation goes to: Linda Hargis, Dawn Harbin, Larry Coleman, nm Pettibone, Linda Harrell, Holly Henson, Debbie O'Connell, and Susan Palko. We are also indebted to the students, staff, and principal Jerry Morton of the Alternative Center for Learning.

PREFACE TO THE SECOND EDITION

This second edition adds new material on migrant children, an alternative school in a small rural county, family resource centers in rural areas of a southern state, and material that assesses what has transpired regarding dropouts since 1990, and the publication of the first edition of *Dropouts.*

R.F.K. and C.H.H.

ACKNOWLEDGMENTS
TO THE SECOND EDITION

We want to express our thanks to Hank McGhee, Edward Headlee, and Gary Dutton, respectively, Assistant Superintendent, Superintendent, and former supervisor of secondary education of Loudon county schools. They were largely responsible, along with Bud Burger, an able communitarian, for establishing Chestnut Ridge Learning Center. Chestnut Ridge Learning Center is an alternative high school for at-risk youth. Its success has been a gratifying affirmation of the principles expressed in this book. We would like to thank Betsy Johnson for typing the new material in this book.

CONTENTS

DROPOUTS

Part 1

An Educational Perspective

Chapter 1

PERSPECTIVE

Each of the authors brings to the dropout problem a different perspective. One has the view of a human service worker. The other, that of a teacher. In examining the problem over the years, we formed images of the problem that synthesize our different points of view. These perspectives influenced the image of what these students look like and how they become dropouts. It also influenced the shape of the model for action that we advocate.

We feel that one must know who these students are and how they come to drop out in order to intervene with reasonable expectation of success. Figure 1 helps to show who the students are and the routes they take either to complete or to drop out of school.

Soon after students start school, they find themselves moving along in separate portions of the curricular path. Higher-achieving students follow one side of the path and lower-achieving students the other.

The portion of the path occupied by higher-achieving students is smooth and relatively free of obstacles. However, the part of the path traveled by the low-achieving students is full of barriers that disrupt progress all along the way. Actually, the curricular path is the same for both groups of students, and herein resides the problem. What some students find reasonably difficult others find frustrating. The curriculum is laid out in normative steps. Most students will find it manageably difficult. Some will find it extremely easy. Others will find it causes only failure. Much more will be said of the link between the lock-step curriculum and dropping out of school in this book. We feel that this is a primary contributing factor for the majority of students who drop out.

We believe that most dropouts should be viewed as curriculum casualties rather than as casualties of personal, family, or financial problems. We do not deny that these latter problems exist in many of these students and may well be contributing factors, but they are primary factors with only a minority of the dropouts. We believe that we have, for too long a time, looked for problems within the dropout and have avoided looking

THE MAP OF GETTING THROUGH SCHOOL: GRADUATE OR DROPOUT

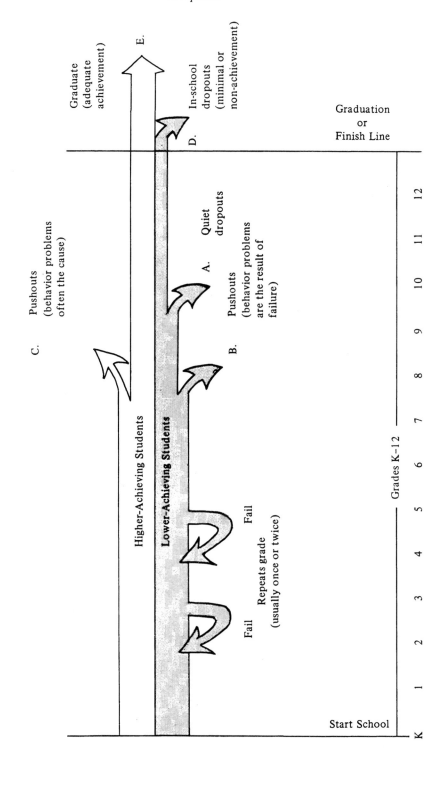

for the cause within the system from which they drop. We have a tendency to blame the victim. We avoid thinking of our schools as victimizers.

An enormous unappreciated range of readiness and learning apptitude characterizes the students who begin school each year. Too often, we treat the extremes of individual variation in students as maladies to be cured. We attempt to cure them by forcing students to fit the rigid forms of our lock-step curriculum. In this process, we cause failure which is the primary obstacle the low-achieving student encounters during her or his school experience. Chronic failure experience eventually produces in many of these at-risk students the many behavior problems that ultimately come to be associated as causes of dropping out rather than as symptoms.

The failure begins almost immediately with many low-achieving students. With sufficient failure a student will be retained and repeat a grade in elementary school. It is a common characteristic of students who will drop out to have failed and repeated one or more grades. In our illustration we show how failure recycles students in the curricular sequence. This recycling process is one factor that makes it difficult to identify accurate figures for dropout rates. Because many students who start in any given year will fail one or more grades, they may be in school extra years and cannot be counted with their original classmates.

We believe that dropouts should be subclassified into at least four groups. The first, and largest group, is composed of the quiet dropouts. These are represented by the arrow labeled "A" on the diagram. Later on in the book they are called "invisible" dropouts because they go unnoticed until they have dropped out. These students are low achievers who experience continued failure through most of their time in school. With virtually no opportunity to experience success in schoolwork and no prospects for successful completion, they drop out after they reach an age at which time it is legal to do so. Their reaction to chronic failure is not overt and attention getting. Their primary distinguishing characteristic is their stoicism.

Group B students are also low achievers whose academic learning abilities are sufficiently out of synchronization so that they are failing almost continually. They, like group A students, often fail and repeat grades and courses, but these students are distinct from group A because of their overt reaction to chronic failure. They react to failure in disruptive, annoying ways. They call attention to themselves continually and are very noticeable. They avoid failure situations by avoiding school. Attendance problems before the legal age to leave school is truancy. These students are in trouble on either or both counts. Suspension and expulsion are the means by which these students are purged or pushed out of the system. They are punished for their behavior while in school and they are punished if they try to avoid school.

Group C usually has the smallest membership. It is made up of students who have adequate or above academic potential. Their behavior or truancy is not the result of lack of ability or from failure. The students who have high academic potential and creativity may find themselves at odds with rigid curriculum structure. They may find the course work boring and without relevance to them. It may be too easy and be more like busywork, or they may have personal, financial or family problems that are primary reasons for their problems in school. Some of these students have had their achievement progress squelched by poor attendance or disruption in the educational process not of their own making. They may be members of transient or migratory worker families. They may have health problems that interfere with regular attendance. The primary cause of the problems of these students is varied, but, since the source of their problems resides outside of school, the best approach to dealing with them is likely through human services rather than through the educational system.

Group D students usually are not formally considered dropouts. We feel that in many respects they are dropouts, in that they have dropped out of learning though they physically remain in school. They are students with lower academic achievement potential. They are out of synchronization with the academic demands of the curriculum. Little achievement progress is made because the work they encounter is frustratingly difficult and seldom permits them to succeed. Even more unfortunate for them, they will seldom achieve up to their academic potential. In spite of the continued failure these students experience, they have somehow managed to continue to attend school.

Group D students usually survive continued poor performance and failure because of compensating factors. They may have compensatory skills that make them want to stay in school, such as an athletic ability that both attracts them to school and provides some opportunity to experience success. Some students simply have a higher tolerance for failure experiences. They have a more durable, self-contained character that inures them to assaults on their self-concept. Some become skilled at masking or hiding their shortcomings or become adept at cheating their way through failure barriers. Some may actually graduate despite deficiencies in achievement. Others will only receive certificates of attendance.

Group E is constituted of the surviving students. Group E students are those whose academic ability fits the form of the lock-step curriculum. They fit, so they do well and achieve to their potential or to levels accepted by the normative standards of the schools.

Most of the dropouts or pushouts are casualties of the lock-step curriculum. However, there are a significant number that are the casualties of problems outside the school. We will spend some time in several of the chapters in showing how these two groups of students can be separated. This is important because one group is treated most effectively by curricular or educational changes and procedures. The other group will need careful educational attention, but, in addition, they need some form of human service intervention.

The clearest illustration of the distinction between the two groups of students appears when the pushout-type student is referred and then placed in a special program. Incidentally, the pushout student is the only group that will receive special attention. This attention will be granted because of the disruptive behavior exhibited by these students. The programs these students may find themselves in are for learning disabled/behavior disordered students or alternative learning center types for students who have been suspended or expelled. Sometimes the programs are hybrid combinations. At any rate, after the students find themselves in such placements, they will typically receive some kind of educational evaluation and be given an education program that is adjusted to their individual ability levels. The effect of doing this is usually obvious, and occasionally dramatic changes are noticed. The behavior of students who are curriculum casualties changes to normal acceptable types in short order. Failure and frustration, the cause of the behavior problem, are removed and so the unacceptable behavior ceases. However, if the cause of the problem behavior is outside the curriculum, the problem will persist despite curriculum change. The two groups are best diagnosed and separated by this kind of conservative educational appraisal.

Individualization of the instructional difficulty level of work assigned to students is the fundamental assessment and intervention strategy for use with pushout students. If problem behavior persists, however, then the cause of the behavior must be determined by further evaluation.

These causes will require direct attention. We have considerably more to say about both intervention strategies in subsequent chapters.

We do not mean to intimate that these students are best handled in alternative and special programs. Certainly this will continue to permit us to overlook the quiet dropout. We are stating that these conservative measures that make special and alternative programs work should be a part of regular education. The dropout problem is in no way an insoluble one. It will not take any new infusion of cash or special programs or materials to solve. The solution is difficult, nonetheless. It requires a major change in the way we regard the curriculum and the way students must fit it. Basically, it is this: The curriculum must be fitted to individual students, not students to the curriculum.

Alternative programs and special education programs may in fact be an obstacle to the real reform needed to prevent dropouts. These programs are safety valves that are supposed to handle students that do not fit curricular expectations and standards. They may actually legitimize, in the minds of many, the curriculum and the failure and casualties its lock step produces. Since these programs exist, it means that students who can't fit should go there.

Even if we had alternative and special education programs for all the group B and C students, we would still be neglecting the majority of the students who will eventually drop out. These are the students who go about their dropping out quietly and without disruption. And still overlooked will be those many students who hang on, but not in terms of achievement.

We will attempt to do two things in this book: review prevailing views and intervention strategies, and then concentrate on our own conservative views and techniques for dropout prevention.

Chapter 2

CURRICULAR CAUSES

In the first chapters a variety of behaviors and environmental characteristics of dropouts were described. The focus of study on this problem so far has been on the dropout and his background. In this chapter, the focus is not on the dropout but on the schools from which he will drop out or be forced to leave. It is our contention that the factor which contributes most to this problem is not within the dropout or potential dropout but in the schools from which they drop. More precisely, this factor is the curriculum. The curriculum defines the way schools are organized and instruction is delivered. Curricular organization determines the way students are evaluated and the ratio of success to failure that results. When a student drops out of school, a curriculum is virtually always a factor. It can be the primary factor or it may be a contributing factor, but it is always a factor.

One may think of a curriculum as a benign list of educational objectives or skills that make up a course of study. In one sense it may be. However, the scope and sequence of items that make up the typical K–12 curriculum make up a matrix into which students must be fitted. It is in this fitting that the damage occurs, and students drop out or are forced out. Rather than being dropouts, these students are actually better characterized as casualties. The injury inflicted on students in the attempts at fitting them to rigid curricular structures makes them curriculum casualties (Hargis, 1982, 1987).

All of the content which makes up a school's curriculum is laid out in nine-month increments which make up each school year. The three R's curriculum predominates the elementary school years, and content subject areas come to dominate as the students approach the secondary level. Children who have attained the age of six by a prescribed date, usually about October fifteenth, form ranks outside first grade classrooms each autumn. There they must pick up a uniform cadence to march in lock step through the curricular path which is laid out in proscribed increments over each of the next twelve years.

11

Each of the twelve-year's work is laid out in the roughly 180-day increments that make up the school year. All students proceed through each year's work day by day in unison (at least this is hoped to be the case).

The lock-step curriculum is further defined by commercially prepared instructional materials. These materials cover all content subject areas as well as the developmental basal reading and language arts programs. They actually dominate the form of most curricula. They provide the scope and sequence of skills to be presented, the activities to be used, and the instructional methods to present them. They outline and dictate the work to be done hour by hour, day by day. Commercially prepared instructional material reinforces the lock step. It is designed to fit the calendar and the routine schedules of the school day.

There is an assumption that children of the same chronological age group will be able to perform similarly in their designated grade. It is also assumed that the curricular materials assigned to each grade level is of an appropriate difficulty level so that every member of the group can achieve successfully in it. Despite restricting the chronological age range to a single year for each grade, individual differences in ability and rate of achievement vary greatly and they do so quite naturally. It is a fact, verifiable by examining the normative data from popular achievement tests, that the range in reading achievement that exists at the end of each grade level is considerable. By eliminating the bottom 5 percent of the distribution at each grade level, most mildly handicapped students can be removed from consideration (Stone, Cundick, & Swanson, 1988). By eliminating the top 5 percent, the students who could be considered academically talented or gifted can be removed from consideration. Even so an extremely wide range in the norms remains. Consider the norms from the 1970 edition of the *Peabody Individual Achievement Test:* The reading achievement in grade equivalent scores ranges over almost three years at the first grade level, over four years at the second grade, over five years at the third grade, and over six years at the fourth grade. The range continues to increase at each successively higher grade level.

We can expect as routine that there will be normal children who are still non-readers at the end of the first grade while some will be reading at the third grade level. At the end of the second grade, some children will still be reading at the beginning first grade level while some will be reading at the fifth grade level. At the end of the third grade, students will be reading from the high first grade level to the seventh grade level.

And by the end of the fourth grade, the range is from the second to the eighth grade reading levels.

Of course, the average level of achievement for each grade level, by the definition of average, must be at that grade level. However, average is only an arithmetic index. It masks the diversity of actual normal achievement that occurs at every grade level. More importantly, it masks the fact that the range in achievement is actually increasing by more than a year at each grade level. The averages stay the same single-year step apart, but the low-achieving students in each grade will be lucky to make three-quarters of a year's progress, while the higher-achieving members of the same class can achieve more than one-and-one-half year's growth in reading ability.

The organization of schools by grades was an attempt to handle the large numbers of students that entered school in the late nineteenth century with the advent of free public education and mandatory attendance laws. Large school systems needed organizations that could deliver instruction efficiently to large numbers of children (NEA, 1974).

It was soon recognized that all students did not fit this curricular structure. Consequently, this recognition brought about the development of ability grouping and tracking procedures. This was a further attempt to make each group more homogeneous in regard to learning ability. In larger school systems two or more groups or tracks were used. A regular and an advanced class might be set up for each grade level or a slow, middle, and advanced class might be used. These kinds of ability groupings were an attempt to provide instruction to the very wide range of learning abilities that existed in each chronological age group. Still, within each classroom, wide variation in readiness, achievement level, and learning rate persisted. Elementary-level teachers further subdivided the classroom into two or more ability groups.

By and large, these systems have increased the success of schools in terms of the number of students that graduate. Seventy-five percent of students in this country complete high school. Still, the dropout rate is extremely large and in some ethnic and socioeconomic groups it is much higher. Some would argue that many other students have dropped out without leaving school. They are in school but they are making no achievement progress. They are a kind of in-school dropout.

We believe that our persisting dropout problem results from the fact that ability grouping systems are attempts to make students fit existing curricular structures. In the process of making students fit these relatively rigid structures, there are casualties. Ability grouping and tracking have reached about the limit of their capability to manage individual differences in learning ability and rate.

The curriculum organization has been likened to the bed of Procrustes (Hargis, 1987). If the students don't fit the curricular bed, they won't have their height altered by an axe or rack, but they certainly will be battered by failing grades and poor achievement. As was mentioned earlier, instruction is organized for groups. Curricular material is assigned to grades and courses in order to provide group instruction. It is organized in lock-step sequences. The same amount of time is allotted for each student to progress along the curricular path. If a student's current achievement level is too low to take the next step successfully, or if the student's learning rate is too slow, he will fail. Ultimately, he will drop out. This student will become a casualty of the curriculum.

Failure and evidence of failure are virtually always listed prominantly as predictors of dropping out or as among the primary characteristics of those who already have. About 15–20 percent of the students in elementary schools fail every year (Jansky & de Hirsch, 1972; Glasser, 1971). These then become a part of the 25 percent of students who drop out.

When students fail within the lock-step curriculum, the problem is typically viewed as one of the student, not the curriculum. If a student continues to fail after the standard grouping or tracking practices have been used, the student will likely be retained. Even this will be done within the framework of the lock-step curriculum. The student will repeat a grade. The decision for retention usually will be made at the end of a year after which he has failed and made little measurable progress. The student will take a one-year backward lock-step and hopefully pick up the cadence with the younger age group of students.

If failure becomes chronic, students will be subjected to a variety of testing procedures to try to find what is wrong with them. The testing is used typically to identify the problem in the student, classify the student and his problem. This is another means of further grouping and tracking students. This may mean that the new group or track is in some compensatory program or in special education. These testing procedures and programs for the most part are necessary to deal with nonhandicapped students who are simply so out of synchronization with the curriculum that failure is a foregone but unfortunate consequence.

Students who are failing are not making adequate achievement progress. If they fail for a sufficient length of time, their achievement will lag far enough behind their potential for achievement that they will qualify for special education placement. This discrepancy condition leads to the classification of learning disability in many states. The size of the discrepancy and the means of calculating it vary somewhat, but it usually is in the order of one standard deviation between achievement and potential for achievement.

If a student is only moderately out of synchronization with the curriculum, retention may place him in a more comfortable achievement entry position for a time. Remember, however, that the lower-achieving students may be learning at a rate that is 10 to 20 percent slower than their average peers. While these students are progressing, they are doing so more slowly, and eventually they will again be behind the curricular sequence and failing again. However, they have made sufficient achievement progress that no significant discrepancy has emerged, and consequently, they fail and without prospect for any special education intervention. With no prospect for improving their lot and in the face of continued failure and frustration, these students avoid the source of their misery by dropping out as soon as they are able, sometime during the high school years.

The dropout who is a curriculum casualty is the product of the attempt to fit her or him to rigid curricular structures. The lesson in this is that the reverse of this condition is necessary if we are to make significant headway in eliminating the dropout problem. Curricula should be fitted to children, not children to curricula.

In the old subscription schools and in the remaining rural schools that bear some resemblance to them, the curriculum was assigned to individual students. In other words, a student started at his or her point of readiness and progressed along the curricular sequence at the rate dictated by their personal levels of achievement. Aside from the instruction that occurred in the home between parent and child, subscription schools were the most common educational system prior to the establishment of public schools in this country. The subscription school worked this way: A group of parents of school-age children would contribute money for each of their children to employ a teacher to instruct this group of children. The teacher would be required to teach the total age range from 6 to as much as 21. All the students would be in one room, often in a building cooperatively constructed by the same parents. Housing, if not provided as a part of the school, would be managed by a rotating living arrangement with each of the subscribing families. Teachers would work with individual students at whatever level they were capable of performing at and then proceed to the next level when the student demonstrated mastery. Progress was reported to the parents by written accounts describing what the student was learning and what had been mastered. There were no grades of any kind and there was no failure. If there was failure, it was that of the teacher. If parents felt that their children were not making sufficient progress, then it was considered failure on the part of the teacher and that teacher would be in danger of losing his or her job.

Grades

The first marks or grades used were on a percentage scale or a scale of 0 to 100 (NEA, 1976; Milton, Pollio, & Eison, 1986). They came into being primarily as a means of screening the greatly expanding number of applicants to colleges that were a consequence of expansion of public education at elementary and secondary levels. These marks had not been necessary in the subscription school era. Few students went to school, and when they did it was seldom beyond the elementary levels. If students intended to go on, they usually would be required to take an admission or qualifying test to get into an institution. Ulysses S. Grant (1885), in commenting on his subscription school experience and his appointment to West Point, said that he stayed in local subscription schools until he had learned everything that the teachers had to present. This was at age seventeen, at which time he went to West Point to see if he had learned enough to pass the admission's examination.

Grades or marks became related to the graded structure of the curriculum. They became comparative figures by which a student's performance could be ranked against other students in the same grade level. They also were indexes of a student's mastery of the subject matter presented at his or her grade level placement. Grades or marks were now used to determine if a student could pass on to the next grade or to graduate. A fundamental change had occurred. Student evaluation had been a direct report of what he or she had learned; now it was a report of how a student was doing compared to others in his or her grade or the standards of the grade. Grades were now an abstraction. They were only a number, a normative index. They told nothing of the specifics of what curricular items were learned or what the student was working on.

The most insidious consequence (and possibly an unforeseen one) was that children could now fail. The blame for no, or poor, achievement had been shifted from the teacher to the student. The student was marked; the student was now responsible for her or his own achievement progress. The educational system was relieved of much of the responsibility for the hard time that many low-achieving students were having in graded school systems.

This criticism is not meant to imply an unequivocal endorsement of the "good-ole" days before grades. Switches and rods in large quantities were consumed to "motivate" students, but there were a number of things that still do recommend schools without grades.

In the graded schools, one level of instruction was provided for each so-called homogeneous group. However, if, in fact, these groups were homogeneous, as was the intent, there would have been a homogeneous group of marks or grades indicating this uniform performance characteristic. This, however, was not the case. Given one level of instruction, a distribution of scores and grades almost inevitably was obtained on tests and assignments.

Grades gradually took on a life of their own. They became their own purpose for existence. Tests and assignments were given so that a grade could be determined. Even the distribution of grades that invariably occurred when the same test or assignment was given to any classroom full of students came to be well accepted. Teachers now feel that it is necessary to get a wide distribution of scores or grades on a test. They feel a need, indeed, there may even be administrative pressure, to give a wide distribution of grades. Too many high grades means that standards are set too low. Too many high grades means grade inflation. When this occurs they feel that grades have been demeaned and have lost value.

If a single level of instructional difficulty is used with any group or classroom of students, it will produce a variety of learning levels. For example, if a twenty-word spelling list is given to a classroom full of students on Monday, the routine instructional activities conducted through Thursday, and a test on the words given on Friday, it would surprise no one that a wide variety of scores would result. Some students would get all the words correct and some miss quite a number. If the words on the spelling test were of average difficulty for that group of students, then the odds are very good that a normal distribution of scores would be produced by the test.

So goes the typical lock-step instructional activity. It is a fact that a wide distribution of grades and scores that results from any instructional activity is evidence that only one level of instruction and curriculum has been provided. It is also a fact that teachers who give a normal distribution of grades to their students are not attending to the individual differences in learning ability of the students.

Grades make this condition possible. Moreover, they encourage it. A distribution of grades has become necessary. Remember, we must maintain standards. After all, what would grades mean if we didn't use them this way? Never mind that about a quarter of our students will fail because of this notion.

Grades make it alright to fail students. However, failure is evidence that no learning is taking place. Remember, you must practice spelling the word correctly enough times to internalize the correct spelling. One must get practice (that is, correct practice) to learn anything, whether it is an addition fact, a new word in reading, or an algorithm in more advanced arithmetic. If students get things incorrect, they are at risk for learning the wrong answer.

Failing grades are evidence that students are not given work at which they can practice correctly and successfully. They are given work that is too difficult and in which little or no learning can take place.

Grades and grading practices encourage the use of a double standard. We have set up the conditions for higher-achieving students to experience great amounts of success. This is evidenced by high scores and high grades on their work. We make it easy for higher-achieving students to do very well. On the other hand, we make it very difficult for lower-achieving students. The work is always hard, often too difficult, as shown by poor and failing grades. We think, though, that the poor grades will stimulate the failing student to work harder for a higher grade. This is a false assumption (Evans, (1976). The only students who are motivated by grades are those who are already getting good grades. We provide work that can be done with high success for the more able students, and work of great difficulty that produces little or no success for the less able; challenge and struggle for the lower-achieving student, comfort and success for the higher achiever.

Students are given grades, so it is their responsibility to improve. The student must do something to get higher scores and better grades. Alternatively, there is something wrong or deficient in the student, in which case the student will need some special help or remedial assistance. The problem of poor grades and lack of achievement has been sited in the student. The student does it. It is not done to him or her.

In the old ungraded or unclassified system as it was called, students were evaluated to see if they could move on to the next curricular level or topic. With the advent of the lock-step curriculum and grades, the students were required to move along with their grade or group. They were evaluated according to the progress they made on the level of instruction assigned to their grade. If they were not appropriately fitted to the learning requirements of the curricular content, they would fail. The only provision for fitting the curriculum to them was retention. And this was done only after the student had suffered failure. After the student had been retained or held back, he or she would start with a new group, again in unison to see if the fit had been made. Failure and retention—these are the most commonly noted characteristics of dropouts. Remember, however, these things typically happen to students, not because these students are willing participants, but because of the structure of our curricula and grades. Students do not willingly and voluntarily fail. Success in school is reinforcing and motivating. Low-achieving students are simply placed in a no-win situation by our institutionalized system.

Grouping and tracking practices were designed to fit students to the lock-step curriculum so that mass instruction could be efficiently delivered. Failure is evidence of the amount of poor fit. These are students who are out of the tolerance limits of the curriculum (Hargis, 1989). Academic ability in any age group exists on a continuum. The extremes on the continuum are not suited for grouping where one level of instruction is provided to the group. Students in the extreme ends of the curriculum will share more academic ability and achievement characteristics with the students in groups or grades either below or above them.

Students are initially grouped by chronological age. All children who have attained the age of six by a given date during the fall of the year are to start first grade. This places students with their age-mates over no more than about a twelve-month age range. However, this does not restrict the range of academic readiness or achievement.

The range in chronological age in a first grade classroom may be only twelve months, but the range in academic achievement, excluding all exceptional students, will be over 2.5 years, over thirty months. Consider again the normative data from the *Peabody Individual Achievement Test* (the 1970 edition). At the first grade level, excluding the bottom and the top 5 percent achieving students, the grade equivalent scores are 0.5 to 3.4. This is a range of 2.9 years! This is the kind of range in performance and achievement that virtually all first grade teachers can expect every year.

Consider the range in achievement that is reported in the normative data for subsequent years. Again, the top and bottom 5 percent of the students have been eliminated to insure that no exceptional students, either handicapped or academically talented, will be included. At the end of the second grade, the range is from 1.1 to 5.3, or 4.2 years. At the end of the third grade, the range is from 1.9 to 7.1, or 5.2 years. By the end of the fourth grade, the range has increased to from 2.5 to 8.7, or 6.2 years. It is quite evident that the normal range of reading achievement is remarkably wide, and it continues to widen over each succeeding school year.

The wide, and increasingly wider, achievement range at each grade level is masked by using the arithmetic mean to determine what the performance level is for any grade level. Even though the normal variation in performance increases greatly, the averages are figures that show simply a one-year difference between each grade.

It should be noted that the lower-achieving students in each subsequent grade are dropping farther and farther behind the average curricular level assigned to their age-designated grade level. One can see why retention is often only a temporary intervention at best. If a student is held back one or even two years, to match his or her achievement level with the grade-level placement, the match may work temporarily, but learning rates that are slower by 10 to 20 percent will eventually leave the student substantially behind and failing again. This is the reason that retention in one or more grades is a commonly noted characteristic of many students who eventually drop out. Retention is evidence of the extent of mismatch that exists between a student's learning rate and the learning rate demanded by the lock-step curriculum.

We readily accept wide variations in student abilities in many non-academic areas. Great variation is expected in athletic, musical, mechanical, and artistic ability. Great variation is also expected in the rate and time that different students require to attain the same ultimate skill level in any of these areas. We very often are, however, intolerant of the normal variation that always exists in academic aptitude in any group of children. The curricular structure defines our expectations and students must fit these expectations. Consequently, there are casualties.

Failure has profound consequences. Failure is more than just evidence of poor performance. It means that learning is not occurring. Remember, you must get things right in order to learn them. Errors practiced are errors learned. Correct answers should be practiced. High performance levels indicate that appropriate practice is occurring.

When students get wrong answers too often, they even learn different and ineffective approaches to learning activities. They may use random guessing. They may acquire an ineffective helpless attitude toward any instructional task that further contributes to their learning problems. Learned helplessness (Grimes, 1981) is a consequence of continually facing frustratingly difficult work. Learned helplessness will even affect a student's approach to work that is of an appropriate difficulty level and is really doable. Chronic failure makes it continually more difficult for a student to acquire academic skill.

Success, on the other hand, fosters still more success. This phenomenon is known as Matthew effects (Stanovich, 1986; Hargis et al, 1988; Hargis, 1989). The basic notion underlying the Matthew effect is that the rich get richer and the poor get poorer, and that this holds true for learning as well. The more you are able to do makes it possible to do even more. The old adage, "the more you do, the more you can do" is true. A child having acquired some reading skill finds increasingly incidental opportunities to practice reading. The same student has increasing opportunities to practice reading skill in other subject areas in school. The more practice, the better the reading skill becomes. In high-achieving students, the growth rate is almost exponential, as is shown in the range of reading achievement in the normative data on standardized tests.

Matthew effects account for the extremely low achievement of the less able students. Having little success in learning to read provides little opportunity for incidental practice in reading. Without reading skill sufficient to read content subject area material at grade level, the practice that could occur in doing schoolwork is missing. The poor do, indeed, get poorer in reading skill in our graded, lock-step curricular structure.

The reaction to failure is as varied as achievement is. Some few students seem able to harden themselves and endure it with apparent stoicism. The assault on the self-concept of other students, however, is too great to be endured without an emotional or behavioral reaction. Students who must endure chronic failure will experience frustration, anxiety, and fear (Glasser, 1971; Simon & Bellanca, 1976; Hargis, 1987, 1989). In the face of such experience, some children will withdraw and avoid instructional activity. Some more naturally assertive and aggressive students will act out in more aggressive and disruptive ways. Avoidance often means dropping out when a student is old enough. Truancy may in fact lead to being suspended or expelled. Acting-out and aggressive behavior leads also to suspension or expulsion. Even the stoic students who manage to stay in school have dropped out of actual learning. They are, in effect, in-school dropouts. These are the students who have made little achievement progress and are often cited as defective products of our schools. They may have acquired little or no reading skill and have made little achievement in other curricular areas. If these students have relatively pleasant personal characteristics they may get differential treatment (Smith & Dobbin, 1960; Leiter & Brown, 1985). They may actually be promoted and graduate due to benign treatment they receive from their teachers.

The attitude of teachers toward their students is affected by how they regard the curriculum and the grading system. The content of the curriculum that a teacher is charged with presenting takes precedence over the individual ability levels of the students in that teacher's classroom. Students must fit or they will very likely fail. Comments such as the following are quite commonplace to teachers: "Joe won't be able to do the work in your room. Just wait and see." "I don't know why they didn't hold him back another year. He hasn't done one bit of passing work since he's been here." "He's going to fail again. Why don't they just go ahead and put him in special ed?"

These comments make clear that students must fit the curricular structure or else fail. Ultimately, most of these curriculum casualties drop out.

Chapter 3

THE VISIBLE AND THE INVISIBLE

Educators don't seem to be able to identify students who are at risk for dropping out. We don't see these students as potential dropouts before they truly disappear. Is it a problem with our vision or are a significant number of these students invisible? Our hindsight seems quite a lot better. In retrospect, we can usually identify a number of problems that have contributed to making a student drop out, but the only potential dropouts we identify are those with disciplinary and behavioral problems sufficient to call attention to themselves. We know what to look for in predicting which students will drop out. Why then aren't we looking for these things in advance and intervening in some way? The authors believe that we avoid seeing these students because our educational system is not designed to accommodate to their needs.

Our educational system is really only concerned with the visible dropout because of repercussions produced by these students on the society outside of school. These problems cause critics to point at the schools. Schools, on the other hand, are willing to overlook the problems of most students that don't cause disruptions and difficulties while in school. The squeaky wheel gets the immediate attention. In the case of the visible dropout, the squeaking starts in school, the squeaking is observed, and occasionally some intervention is attempted. The reason for the intervention, however, will be to deal with the students' disruptive behavior and not necessarily with the intent of keeping them from dropping out. These students will be on their way to being pushed out.

Both of these groups of students, the visible and the invisible, share important characteristics. The causes of their problems are usually similar. It is that their reaction to the causes is different. In both instances, we need to learn to observe our students with the objective of intervening as the signs of difficulty appear. In this chapter we will deal with the conditions which cause both types of students to drop out. We do this with the view to make the currently invisible student more apparent, at least transluscent, so that changes in the instructional delivery system can be made to keep them in school. We also do this with the intent that the visible dropouts be helped before the characteristics which make them so apparent emerge.

The distinguishing characteristic that makes one group obvious and the other unnoticed is overt behavior. The visible students are so because their behavior is disruptive, annoying, unruly, non-conforming or generally unacceptable in a variety of ways. The invisible students generally act in ways that are within the limits of normal acceptable behavior. Some may be extra quiet, even withdrawn.

Both groups of students have academic problems. It is their reaction to the problem that distinguishes the two groups. Children who are failing seldom are happy. The behavioral reaction to failure is varied, however. When failure is chronic, some students become inured and stoic. Some become aggressive and act out against the source of irritation to their self-concept. Schoolwork becomes a source of pain; so, some students learn to avoid academic activity while in school, and others avoid school altogether through truancy.

There are some exceptions to the above. Students that come from families who are transient, especially those engaged in migrant work, will miss school frequently enough to pose a serious learning problem. Here the problem is the reverse of the one mentioned above. Absence is the cause of the learning difficulty, not the result of it. These students may be out of school enough to make them fall out of synchronization with most curricula, or they may find themselves confronted with new and different curricula that they are not prepared to deal with. These problems feed on each other. Absence causes the migrant student to fall behind. Subsequent failure causes the student to avoid still more. These students find it very easy to drop unnoticed through the cracks. This group of students poses a significant problem alone. These students and their problems are the topic of a later chapter.

The other group of students that is an exception is made up of those who have real learning or behavior problems. With these students, their learning problems are intrinsic to them. Their learning and behavior problems are the cause of their difficulties, not the result of a mismatch with the curriculum. Their problems will be exacerbated by further failure, but fundamentally they will need special attention to remove or ameliorate the interfering behavior or learning problem. This minority of students must be distinguished from the larger group who are simply curriculum casualties.

In an earlier chapter we detailed the assessment procedures for distinguishing students who are curriculum casualties from students who have actual learning and behavior problems. We don't mean to imply that one type of problem is less serious to the student than the other. It is just that the approaches to dealing with them have fundamental differences. Remember, in the first group the curriculum mismatch is really the cause of the problem and so it must get the major attention. In the last group, the learning and behavior problems of the students influence the way they deal with curriculum and instruction. Consequently, the learning and behavior problems themselves must be the focus of instruction. Briefly, the assessment procedure that separates the two groups is this: The students' current level achievement is carefully determined and a specific baseline of skill development is evaluated. Curriculum materials and instructional activities are carefully prepared for use with the students at their individual instructional levels. The students are then engaged in activities and materials for a sufficient length of time to show the effect on their behavior. The behavior and learning problems of the curriculum casualty group will lessen significantly after only a short time. The problem behavior will persist in those students with real disabilities. With this group, a non-curricular cause needs to be identified and/or a disability dealt with specifically. These students may need a special education program where their behavioral disability can become the focus of instruction or where the environment can be controlled well enough for the student to benefit from instruction.

The quiet, or invisible, dropouts fall silently behind. They may be held back in some grades, which permits them to perform adequately for awhile in that temporary grade placement, but they gradually fall behind again. By the time these students reach high school their poor achievement provides them little hope of passing or ultimately graduating. Because of earlier retention, these students may have reached an age where truancy may no longer be a legal issue. Many of the students may be employed, and this makes the avoidance of school much more attractive. Indeed, it may be the best alternative for students who have little chance of making achievement progress given the curricular structure of their schools. There is little to be gained from enduring the pain of attendance under these conditions. If the students have found employment, they are unlikely to return to school. In many respects the students who find employment when they drop out are better off. They are gaining work experience and an employment record. They are able to learn many useful things, whereas they could only hope to learn to cope with failure or learn to be increasingly helpless if they remain in school.

The more visible of the potential dropouts may qualify for alternative educational programs if such are available. When the behavior of students becomes such that they are being suspended or even expelled, some school systems may provide alternative education programs for them in an effort to keep them in school. One such program is described in this book. These programs typically will be successful in keeping students in school while they are assigned to them because they immediately identify students entry-level skills and provide instruction in which the students can succeed. They are less successful in reintroducing the students to the regular educational program because the students will find themselves back in the same frustrating environment that produced the problem behavior in the first place.

Alternative programs are successful while students attend them. However, they are largely designed for the students who would otherwise be forced out of school anyway. The invisible majority will usually not benefit from such programs because their behavior is within socially acceptable bounds. There is, however, one circumstance that is likely to identify the less visible students and qualify them for alternative programming. This is poor attendance or truancy. There is an embarrassing contradiction about suspending or even expelling a student for not going to school. There may be the tendency to try something to keep these students in school.

As was mentioned earlier, students drop out from learning before they actually drop out of school. Some students drop out of learning but manage to stay in school. Somehow they learn coping skills that help them endure the frustration and lack of achievement. These students may have compensatory skills, maybe social or athletic, that assist them in moving along. They are out of synchronization with the curriculum, but they are being carried along with their classmates.

Are these students any better off than the students who drop out of learning and attendance? They probably are, but it will not be because the schools have contributed to their welfare. These students are getting along and managing to get by. Because they are, they won't call much attention to themselves and they are likely to be overlooked. Through the more popular use of minimal competency tests, or proficiency tests, these students have become more noticeable. The number of low-achieving students who remain in school appears to equal the number of students that drop out.

It is not necessary that students be totally out of synchronization with the curriculum in order to drop out. Students without compensatory skills that aid in their survival in school may drop out if they are at the lower margins of achievement. These students need the lift that success provides. A poor self-concept is not enhanced by marginal, even if passable, achievement.

The problems the schools face in dealing with the dropout problem is first in identifying the students who are on their way to dropping out of learning and school. This is a more difficult task than it may seem. Our educational system makes it alright to fail students. Failure is not often viewed as diagnostic information. That is why our system does not do a good job of identifying most students who are at risk for dropping out. If we would use failing grades as our primary screening instrument, most of these invisible individuals would stand out rather prominently.

It is indeed unfortunate that we have such an obvious diagnostic instrument. It is really evidence of our failure to deal fairly with these students. We do, nevertheless, have grades, and poor and failing grades are primary evidence that a student is at risk for dropping out.

However, it would be far better to identify these students before failure occurs. Evidence of problems can be collected by simply observing performance on routine schoolwork. Are students able to do the work assigned to them? Are they able to read their textbooks? Is the work being provided to a given student a reasonable match to his current skill level? Evidence concerning this match can readily be collected by checking the student's work. Instead of checking and scoring work in order to assign a grade, the work is checked to see if it is of an appropriate difficulty level. Certainly any work that warrants a failing grade should be considered too difficult for a student. The appropriateness of texts can be evaluated by using informal inventory procedures. Certainly if a student's comprehension level of a text is 50 percent or less, it is inappropriate. Students compelled to use texts that are beyond their means will not gain in reading skill or gain the information they contain. The details of assessing the students in regard to instructional activity will be covered in a later chapter, but fundamentally the procedures determine if there is a discrepancy between the students' skill and the demand of their classroom. If there is a discrepancy, the student is at risk.

The above procedure is basic for identifying the bulk of the less visible students. Are they able to do the work they are being given? However, there are potential problems even among the students who are at the margins of acceptable achievement. If the self-concept of these students seems diminished, they may well be at risk also. Some students may feel that they lack any compensatory attributes or skills. They may feel they lack in appearance, personality, or talent. Marginal grades may only further devalue these students in their own eyes. If these students find any occupation or activity outside of school that makes them feel more estimable, it may compete to the extent that they drop out.

The intervention most appropriate for these students is very much related to the assessment method used to identify them. This is the modification of their curricular and instructional activities. If their work is observed to be frustratingly difficult or impossible to do, then the work is modified to the point where the student is readily able to do it and feel an acceptable level of success and competence. Major changes and shifts may be needed in the way the curriculum is structured in order to provide this success. Curricula must be assigned to the students according to their needs. It should not be assigned to grades and the students placed there to fit as best they can.

Two student profiles are included next to illustrate the basic distinction between the visible and the invisible dropout:

Fred is nineteen. He did not return to school a year ago after the summer vacation. He was in approximately the tenth grade. He currently holds jobs in two fast-food restaurants. He has no intention of going back to school. However, he wants to start taking some evening classes at the local middle school to help him prepare to take the GED. He wants the diploma so that he might be able to join the military service. Currently, his job schedules interfere with this plan.

Fred was retained in the second grade and repeated the fifth grade when the family moved to another city, where he was tested for placement when enrolling in the new school. Fred's grades remained poor and then turned for the worse in high school. Several of the courses that Fred needed to graduate were too difficult and graduation seemed to be beyond his reach.

Fred was old enough to graduate, but graduation, even if he could pass the hard classes, looked to be years away. He wanted a car very badly; so when working at a summer job in a fast-food restaurant, he arranged to purchase and pay for one from a fellow worker. When it was time to start back to school, Fred found that the obligation for payment, operating costs and repairs on the car would mean that he would have to keep working to keep up with them.

Fred's not attending school that fall was left without much comment by his mother. Neither she nor her former husband had completed high school, and there had never been any firm expectation that her children would either.

Fred had managed to achieve about sixth grade skills in most academic subject areas. Written language skills and arithmetic were lower. Fred has the potential to pass the minimal competency test needed for graduation. His primary obstacles to graduation are in passing the required courses. Fred's behavior has always been quiet and cooperative given the limits of his academic ability. Fred was never considered a discipline problem at school, and he is considered a good employee wherever he works. With some assistance with language arts and math, Fred should be able to get his GED.

Fred has a number of real assets. It is too bad that the curriculum was not sufficiently flexible to capitalize on them. If he is to get a diploma, it will have to be outside the regular educational system. It may be true that Fred dropped out, but it seems more as though he were excluded.

Fred represents the majority of students that drop out. He caused the system no significant hardship or annoyance. His passing was scarcely noticed. His problems with the system were a source of pain primarily to himself. For this reason, Fred remained essentially invisible until after the fact.

Derron, on the other hand, is a representative of a visible minority:

Derron is 18. He dropped out of school last year after spring break. Derron had been certified as having a significant behavior disorder and had received special education services for about a year and a half, after which time he was judged ready to go back into regular classroom. He had been back in regular tenth grade classes for less than three months when he dropped out.

Derron's records show that, since the second grade, he had been repeatedly disciplined for his unruly behavior. His parents had been routinely contacted about his disruptive behavior. Derron had become more aggressively disruptive when moved to middle school. Minor acts of vandalism on school property and the possessions of other students increased. His aggressive behavior was characterized as dangerous and impulsive. He had been in trouble for swearing, hitting, and fighting. He was finally referred for special education evaluation when two of his teachers insisted that they could no longer tolerate his uncooperative and disruptive behavior in their classrooms.

Derron's parents were cooperative, but their efforts had been ineffective at improving his in-school behavior. They were at a loss to account for his behavior there since his behavior seemed alright at home. In fact, his relatives and neighbors were always surprised to hear that Derron would behave in such a way at school. It was nothing like what they witnessed in the home or neighborhood.

Derron worked as a busboy part time while in school and has worked full time since he dropped out. He has been a valued employee and his employer was surprised to hear that Derron had been in a class for behavior disordered students and, later, that he had dropped out.

Derron's academic achievement is at close to seventh grade levels in all subject areas. He has passed the proficiency test and could have graduated if he had managed to stay in school. Derron's achievement level surprised his teachers, since they claim he never paid attention in class and never completed any homework assignments. His mother, commenting on his poor performance in class and with his homework, said that she had tried to make him do his homework but never could. When she tried to help him do it, she found the tasks too difficult and so was never of any assistance.

Derron's special classroom teacher had a very different attitude toward him. She said he had never posed any problems to her at all. In fact, she said she wished that all her students had no more problem than Derron had. The only possible behavior problem that Derron had shown in her room was some sulkiness and withdrawal when he first arrived. She added that this is to be expected when a student is placed in her room, since they believe it is a form of punishment.

She further stated that Derron soon found that her classroom wasn't all that bad after all. She said that she never tolerates any aggressive behavior in her classroom and she insists that all the students do their work. She went on that this really wasn't much of a problem in her room anyway with most of her kids. The first thing she does is identify some entry-level skills and then start instruction wherever the student happens to be. She had never had any trouble getting Derron to do his work because she never gave him any work that he couldn't get done.

While Derron was in the special class, he prepared for and passed the proficiency test. The change in his behavior was so marked and his academic progress so obvious that it was decided to put him back in the regular school program. Within three months Derron had dropped out.

His special classroom teacher commenting on this stated sadly, "This unfortunately happens too often when they try to return my students to the regular classroom. The administration thinks I have cured the kids when I haven't done anything but change the environment so that it doesn't make them crazy. They are put back in the old environment and the same old behavior that got them in trouble returns. Derron couldn't deal with it any better than before, so he just dropped out."

Derron's problems in school were a source of pain not only to himself but to his regular classroom teachers. His behavior in the regular classroom made him far more visible than students like Fred. The dropping out of students like Derron is usually noted with relief by their teachers.

Derron shares with Fred the problem of finding help outside the school's structure. Derron clearly has the ability to make achievement progress sufficient to attain the GED. One only hopes that he will identify the resources that will assist him in working toward passing the GED test. He is now pretty much on his own.

With either type of student, the schools need to accommodate to meet their needs. If we do not, the students will continue to drop out. Our current practice is to attempt to change the students so that they accommodate to our needs. We overlook the reasons for and the consequences of failure. It is only when the student's behavior becomes annoying or disruptive as a result of continued failure that we pay any attention, and then we usually attempt to alter the symptomatic behavior rather than dealing with the cause. This approach is never effective if failure is the root cause of the problem. If failing grades is the lens used to search for potential dropouts, most will have a substantial image.

We need to recognize the importance of failing grades as diagnostic indicators of children who are at risk for dropping out. In most cases they also provide direct evidence of what should be done to help a student. The curriculum should be adjusted to permit the student to succeed. The adjustment itself provides the next important step in the diagnostic process for students with behavior problems. Does the behavior persist even after the adjustment is made? If it does, then the behaviors, their cause, and their change should be the focus of special education activity. At this stage of assessment, we should have left only a small minority of the at-risk students. The majority's problems will have been solved by the curricular adjustments.

Chapter 4

NEEDED CHANGES
IN INSTRUCTIONAL DELIVERY

Assessment

A fundamental change in assessment procedures is necessary if we are to manage the dropout problem. The current uses of assessment emphasize labeling and grading. Neither of these contributes much information that aids at-risk students. The approach to assessment that we advocate is called curriculum-based assessment (Gickling & Thompson, 1985; Tucker, 1985; Hargis, 1987).

With curriculum-based assessment (CBA), assessment is used for avoiding failure and for programming the success of students. Tests provide information on where students should begin instruction, and should provide direct guidance in planning daily instructional activities. Tests, as they are currently used, do not do this. They exist quite independent of the curriculum and the instructional delivery system used to impart the curricular objectives. Currently, tests are of no help in meeting the daily instructional routines. They actually are factors which contribute to the dropout problem.

Norm-referenced tests constitute the bulk of published tests. Norm-referenced means that the tests have been given to groups representing certain populations. These populations may be organized by geographic area, grade level, ethnic or socioeconomic characteristics, etc. With norm-referenced tests, individuals can be compared with the norms, or a group's performance can be compared with normative groups that have been constituted similarly.

Norm-referenced tests have little relevance to the needs of students during routine instruction (Shriner & Salvia, 1988; Jenkins & Pany, 1978). They just don't have enough items from any curricular area or level to provide meaningful information as to what the specific skill level or needs of specific students are. A more serious criticism is that the items sampled from each level and area don't correspond to the things actually being presented in the schools. In other words, standardized achievement tests are lacking in content validity. Consequently, norm-referenced tests have very limited utility for students at risk for dropping out. They have some use in screening students to prevent them from having difficulties in school, but, unfortunately, their results are most often referred to after the fact.

One type of norm-referenced test that can be used in this preemptive fashion is the readiness test. Readiness tests may lack accuracy in predicting specific levels of academic achievement in students, but they can predict failure quite well (Hargis, 1982, 1987). However, these tests will miss some students who are at risk for failure because of reasons other than academic readiness. These reasons include things related to family, community, and health and will need measuring techniques in addition to readiness tests. These other problems are determined by teacher inquiry, questionnaires, and observation.

Heading off failure is the most important function of testing. It represents the best use of standardized tests. However, this is only a screening function. Tests should be the signal used to identify at-risk students. They determine if a student is ready to begin academic instruction. They should be used to see if the students have reached a stage of achievement which will permit them to succeed at the next level on the grade and curriculum sequence.

This preemptive use of tests is different than their current use. Now, results are typically used only after failure is a fact. Unfortunately, failure, itself, is our primary screening device. This must change.

Most testing that goes on in classrooms is for the purpose of giving grades. Testing for grades is routine. Tests may be given after units of work are completed. They may be given weekly. They are usually given at the middle and end of terms during the school year. The tests are often teacher made, but they are also frequently supplied with the instructional programs in use. Assuming that the tests are valid samples of the curriculum content which has been presented, the students' performance on them will reflect how much of the curricular content so sampled has been acquired. Since the test will represent the single level of items sampled from a lock-step curriculum, the students' performance on these tests will be predictably varied. If by chance a teacher gives a test made with items that are too simple, then the grade variation is reduced. Too many students will get high scores. The teacher will have to make a harder test or be more discriminating (picky) in the way the test is graded.

Policy guidelines are often provided by schools or school systems concerning the grading system. They usually are percentage scales that look something like this: Ninety-three to one hundred equals an A. Eighty-five to ninety-two equals a B. Seventy-seven to eighty-four equals a C. Seventy to seventy-six equals a D. Zero to sixty-nine is an F.

If a teacher has a class representing a normal range of ability, a test prepared from the curriculum for that grade might even produce the "ideal" distribution of grades. This is the 6-22-44-22-6 distribution of grades under the normal curve (Cureton, 1971); that is, 44 percent C's, 22 percent each for B's and D's, and 6 percent each for A's and F's.

Individual teachers may be reluctant to give tests that produce so little high performance. They may prepare somewhat easier tests or score the tests in more generous ways. They may give students bonus points or give extra credit assignments. Such teachers may be accused of contributing to grade inflation if they are overly generous. However, whatever the teachers do to help the students here, the purpose is to manipulate grades. These things have little to do with real instruction and measurement. All of this measurement and manipulation has to do with giving grades.

Testing should not be done to give grades. Testing should be done to find out where a student is on the curricular ladder so that instruction can commence at an appropriate level of difficulty. Routine assessment should be conducted to evaluate the appropriateness of materials and instruction for the student. In other words the materials and instruction should be graded or evaluated, not the student.

We know that high performance levels are associated with the best achievement. Mastery is usually measured in a range of 90 to 100 percent accuracy. Levels of accuracy associated with the instructional level range from 70 to 90 percent (Hargis, 1987; Gickling & Thompson, 1985). These percentages are the figures that we want to maintain for each student. Instructional materials and activities must be adjusted to produce these figures.

There are several reasons why high performance levels must be maintained. The first is a basic learning issue. In any drill or practice activity, the correct answer or response must be associated with each item a sufficient number of times in order to learn it correctly. For example, to learn the addition fact 3 + 5, the number 8 must be associated with it a sufficient number of times to fix the combination in permanent memory storage. Similarly, in order to master a sight word (common unphonetically spelled words), the correct spoken word must be associated with its printed counterpart with sufficient repetition in order that the word be instantly recognized. In both cases, correct repetition is critical. You must get the right answer enough times to learn the right answer.

High accuracy levels on drill or practice activities are evidence that correct answers are being learned. Low performance levels indicate that too many wrong answers are being associated with the items. If low performance levels are permitted, learning wrong answers is encouraged. High performance levels are necessary for the student to benefit from practice, but they are also important to prevent learning error patterns or ineffective guessing strategies which eventually require remedial attention.

In reading instruction or any activity which requires reading, high performance levels should also be in evidence. The standard for instructional level performance was posed by Emmett Betts (1946). If reading material is appropriate in difficulty for instructional use, students should be able to accurately identify 96 percent of the words and have at least 75 percent comprehension over the material's content. If the reading material is for independent use, the students should have a 90 percent comprehension level and accurately identify more than 98 percent of its words.

High accuracy and performance levels are important for learning efficiency, but just as important is the fact that instructional level tasks permit maximum engagement in them. When task difficulty exceeds the difficulty level outlined for the instructional level, students spend less time engaged in actually doing and benefitting from them.

Time fruitfully engaged in learning activities is directly related to achievement (Rosenshine & Berliner, 1978; Gickling & Thompson, 1985). This, therefore, is another very important reason to insure high performance levels in tests and instructional activities. High performance levels permit and encourage academic learning time.

Time not engaged in learning is not productive time. When a student is not engaged in a learning activity, he will be engaged in something else. It may be a behavior that is demanding on teacher time. It may be disruptive to the classroom. It may be quiet withdrawal. It is per se not productive.

High performance levels are also direct evidence to both students and teachers that instruction has been a success. Success itself, however, is an important ingredient in achievement. Success is an important and powerful reinforcer (Skinner, 1972). Success must be planned by using assessment to evaluate instructional activities to insure instructional-level performance. Assessment should not be used simply to supply grades. It should be used to tune the difficulty level of instructional activities and materials to students so that they can perform with success.

Instructional-level performance by students is certainly motivating to them, but it is also motivating to teachers. There is probably nothing so dear to a teacher's heart as having students engaged in learning, completing their work, and doing so successfully. It is also highly motivating to teachers to keep their students engaged in learning. Dealing with off-task behavior is fatiguing and demoralizing. Assessment that is used to provide instructional-level activities to students is fundamental to good classroom management and the management of student behavior.

The essence of curriculum-based assessment is that it is an intrinsic part of ongoing instructional activity. Any activity or assignment is used as a test. A student's performance level on any activity is assessed. Has the activity produced instructional-level performance? Any assignment that can be graded can be judged instead for its match with student skill level. A math worksheet, a turn at oral reading, a spelling test, most routine activities can be used to assess a student's performance on them. The student's performance on the activities is judged in view of making an adjustment in difficulty level. These activities are not simply marked with a red pencil, the marks tallied, and the results entered in a grade book. Performance is used to see if the instructional-level match has been made.

Curriculum-based assessment makes testing part and parcel of the curriculum. Test items should be aligned with the actual curriculum used in a particular school (Archbald & Newmann, 1988). Real achievement progress can most accurately be gauged in this way. Standardized achievement tests do not accurately assess the specifics of any particular curriculum. With tests that are curriculum based, entry level or current skill levels of students can be determined and instructional activity matched to this level. Routine instructional activities are used as assessment devices. Remember, any activity that can be graded can be used in this way. This ongoing assessment activity is the front line of CBA. It is how the instructional-level match is maintained, and academic learning time is optimized. Curriculum-based assessment requires that success be the focus of assessment and instructional activity. It intimately ties assessment to instruction. Unfortunately, current assessment practices do none of this. Assessment is often isolated from ongoing instruction.

When students fail enough times to draw attention to themselves, they may be subjected to diagnostic tests to determine what the cause of their difficulty is. However, diagnostic tests are no more likely to sample skills presented on any particular curriculum than are standardized achievement tests. Some diagnostic tests measure hypothetical contructs that are assumed to be related to achievement difficulties. These constructs include things like visual or auditory perception (not to be confused with visual or auditory acuity), learning style, cognitive processing, etc. Giving these tests to students who are experiencing failure will often cause the students extra problems. Invariably, these students will demonstrate deficiencies on some portion of these tests. This leads to the conclusion that this deficiency needs remediation. If a remedial program is prescribed for the students based on the deficit, it will constitute another curriculum that will compete with the primary one. These will be at odds. The student who needs time and remediation on the regular curriculum will actually get less time for this because of the new curriculum.

These kinds of remedial efforts based on such diagnostic tests are often more than just ineffective; they actually are detrimental, in that they divert attention from the real problem. Diagnostic tests should be made of the specific sequence of skills that make up the curriculum in use. Skills deficiencies on that curriculum are most likely the culprit in the student's academic problems.

There are diagnostic measures that should be used that are likely to have a valid relationship with student achievement even though they are not curriculum based. These include vision and hearing tests, inventories of student's health and nutritional condition, and family and social status.

Making the match between students and instructional activities provides the opportunity for an important assessment procedure. The match must be made in order to determine if a student is failing and at risk for dropping out for reasons other than the curriculum. The students' precise achievement level on the curriculum is determined, ongoing instructional activities are prepared, and their use with the students is monitored to insure that the match is maintained.

This assessment activity is essential to see if a student's poor performance is the result of a curricular mismatch or the result of a problem within the student or his background. If, after a few days of being provided carefully matched instruction, a student's problems persist, then a non-curricular cause is involved and needs to be identified.

Even if non-curricular causes are found, it in no way alleviates the teachers' obligation to maintain the instructional-level match. A mismatch can profoundly exacerbate the difficulties of students with other problems that affect learning. The condition of the vast majority of at-risk students will be greatly improved if the match is maintained, and, in most cases, no other treatment will be required.

Ongoing assessment activities needed to make the match between instructional difficulty level and student achievement level are informal. Student performance on routine work and assignments is observed or monitored. This monitoring should be constant. The effort is not greater than that required for scoring or evaluating for grades. Its purpose is entirely different, however. Instruction is being evaluated, not students. Much failure and many subsequent problems could be avoided.

Instruction

With curriculum-based assessment, assessment becomes an integral part of ongoing instructional activity. It is a necessary function of curriculum-based assessment to insure that students have continuing success in learning activities. The implementation of curriculum-based assessment changes the role of the teacher. Instruction becomes student centered rather than teacher centered. The multilevels of student ability in every classroom precludes the normal teacher-centered delivery system. The teacher's role becomes increasingly that of an observer and monitor of student performance. The teacher must become a facilitator of student success. Consequently, the student not the teacher is the central character in the classroom.

The teacher can no longer dominate classroom time, lecturing and demonstrating. Students cannot be engaged in learning activities when teachers are engaged in lecturing. Pollio (1984) found that at best students are attending to lecture only a little more than 50 percent of the time. Those students who are at lower levels of achievement than that required for the lecture topic will be engaged in the subject hardly at all. The teacher may demand the appearance of rapt attention, but the students cannot focus their real attention if the lecture is over their heads.

Far more classroom time must be given over to activities where the student is engaged in learning and the teacher attending. When the student is engaged, the teacher can moniter his or her performance to see if the instructional match has been made. If it has not, then the teacher will modify the activity, find new material to use, and provide the necessary helpful feedback to make certain that the student is not practicing errors. The student remains engaged and experiences sufficient success so that maximum achievement will occur.

The bulk of classroom time is for the student to be engaged in learning activities and the teacher observing, monitoring, facilitating, and finding and preparing materials. When students are so engaged, the consumption of instructional materials is far greater than in regular classroom organizations (Topping, 1988). The teachers' role is virtually reversed if curriculum-based assessment is implemented. That is, the students become the principle players and the teacher becomes the audience. The teacher's role is not passive, however. Teachers should constantly be engaged in assessing and facilitating learning.

It is obvious that the use of curriculum-based assessment will require the individualization of instruction. This requires a markedly different classroom organization than that typically found in systems committed to lock-step curricula.

The transition to an individualized instructional delivery system may seem overwhelming to many teachers whose only model for instruction has been teacher centered. They believe that the model for excellent teaching is the classroom in which a marvelously interesting and dynamic teacher lectures enthusiastically. The students sit enraptured, their attention riveted to every detail. All students readily follow the verbal map the teacher is laying out, with only an occasional question being raised because a phrase was masked by peals of appreciative laughter or other sympathic vocalization.

Such classrooms exist largely in our imagination. It is a model we cling to, however. What we really find in our heterogeneous world of students are differences in ability as diverse as the grades awarded to them. Actual classrooms, especially at the secondary levels where classrooms are organized around narrow content subject areas, are something more like this: The teacher has sorted out the students who understand what is going on in the course. The lectures are directed to these students. The seating arrangement may even reflect the different ability levels. If the teacher has not made the arrangement, the students will likely have moved themselves if they were free to do so. The teacher is largely responsive to the students who fit within the ability level needed to stay on task in this curricular niche. The students who do not fit are left out for the most part, and the teacher's usual interaction with them will be for the purpose of dealing with disruptive or annoying behavior. For these students who are not able to cope with the difficulty level of the course content, this classroom will be a deadly bore. Not being able to be engaged in or benefit from the instructional activities, these students will be left to their own devices as how best to occupy their time. Some of these students quietly withdraw into themselves. Others will seek out diversion.

These students will not feel valued in this classroom, and they will be right. They may feel, consequently, that there is no reason to show respect and obedience where there will be no reciprocation. This environment contributes to the demoralization of both students and teacher.

How can we change? How can we begin to assign the curriculum to students rather than grades in order that they progress along the curricular path at their own pace, succeeding at each step along the way? Admittedly, it is hard to change given the institutionalized practices of assigning the curriculum to grades and then assigning grades to students. Is it possible to change the whole system? Can individual teachers implement a student-centered curriculum in the midst of such rigid institutionalized practices? These are hard questions, but the answers exist as do the practices which confirm their practicality.

Alternative learning centers such as the one described in this book are examples of programs that are student centered. Rural schools with multigrade classrooms provide other good examples. Special classrooms and resource rooms are also examples of programs where multiple levels of ability are served within the same room.

The instructional activities that must go on in a student-centered environment can be quite varied. They include independent study, supervised study, peer tutoring, and cooperative learning. A substantial body of literature supports usefulness of peer tutoring and cooperative learning activities (Topping, 1988, 1989; Uttero, 1988; Stevens et al., 1987; Slavin, 1987, 1983; Glasser, 1986).

Peer tutoring and cooperative learning arrangements have some important components for use with students at risk for dropping out. The cooperative rather than competitive component is very important. Helping, social interaction is required. The paired tutoring relationships and the cooperative teams of four or five students focus on the success of all members. Everyone is supposed to do well by plan. The amount of time engaged in learning is vastly increased.

Cooperative learning activities generally go something like this: After initial instruction by the teacher, students work together on practice activities until each student gets the correct answers. The students discuss the answers, reach concensus, drill each other, and assess one another to make certain that each member of the group will demonstrate mastery when assessed individually by the teacher.

The success of each member of the team requires cooperation. Extra incentives, other than the intrinsic ones, may be used to encourage all students to do well and to help their teammates. As students provide one another with explanations of concepts or skills, they themselves gain in achievement. In the act of helping, learning is enhanced in the helper. This cycle of cooperative learning significantly increases student achievement.

In addition to achievement gains, cooperation rather than competition has direct benefits for students. Cooperative learning eliminates chronic failure experience. With this, the students can gain normal levels of confidence and self-esteem. An environment that expects and assists all students to do well is a place where a student feels accepted and secure.

Cooperative learning arrangements greatly improve the quality of what are called "follow-up" activities. For example, it is a common practice when a teacher is working with one reading group to have the students in the other reading groups working on activities that take little teacher supervision. These are the "follow-up" activities. Research on these follow-up activities suggests that they are often of poor quality. They are seldom integrated with other reading activities, and the time actually spent on task during follow-up activities is quite low (Stevens et al., 1987). Additionally, in a classroom with three reading groups, about two-thirds of reading time is used for follow-up activities.

Follow-up activities take on far more importance and usefulness if cooperative learning is used. The quality of follow-up time is the most important part of reading instruction. It is the largest time segment devoted to reading instruction, and it should be effective engaged time. Remember, achievement is a function of the amount of engaged time. Students in pairs or groups of four or five can be engaged and assisted far more effectively by peers than they could in a competitive environment with only the teacher to help. In the cooperative setting, the students who are providing the help are also benefitting from time engaged in the activity.

The amount of helpful corrective feedback increases greatly and further enhances the quality of the engaged time. Most drill activities occur in follow-up time. The quality of drill is also greatly enhanced in the cooperative setting because the student is permitted to make few errors without correction. Doing well, getting things right is the purpose of cooperative learning activity.

Students who are failing in competitive grade-oriented programs need cooperative learning approaches to keep them from failing and ultimately dropping out. Competition is only motivating for those students who have sufficient skill to be competitive. Grades are motivating only to those who can get good grades. The students who are at risk for dropping out are demoralized in academically competitive classrooms.

In competitive programs, there is often a strong temptation to cheat. When students realize that there is little hope for doing well, it seems the only option. There is little temptation to cheat in settings where everyone is supposed to do well, and everyone is supposed to help everyone else to do well. Cheating is not an issue in genuinely cooperative learning environments.

Cooperative learning with curriculum-based assessment procedures make an excellent, mutually enhancing combination. Success for every student is the principle aim of each.

The importance of success and failure to achievement is illustrated in the previously discussed phenomena called Matthew effects (Stanovich, 1986; Hargis et al., 1988). The concept of Matthew effects comes from the Gospel according to Saint Matthew.

> For whosoever hath, to him shall be given, and he shall have more abundance: but whosoever hath not, from him shall be taken away even that he hath. (XIII:12)

> For unto everyone that hath shall be given, and he shall have abundance: but from him that hath not shall be taken away even that which he hath. (XXV:29)

Basically, Matthew effects are "the rich get richer, and the poor get poorer" phenomenon. The more effectively you can engage in any activity, the better you can get at it. This is true to the limits of one's talent. It is as true of school learning as it is of learning to play golf, to play a musical instrument, or to be a mechanic. The opposite is also true.

If you engage in an activity ineffectively or poorly, you will probably not improve and may even get worse.

In learning to read, for example, as students acquire reading skill, opportunities for reading open all around them. Print information is everywhere. Reading is in all the subject areas at school. Many opportunities for additional practice at reading occur all the time. The students who are succeeding begin succeeding at quickening rates. The more the students can read, the more reading is done, and still more able readers the students become.

On the other hand, if students are failing or doing very poorly, they are apt to drop farther and farther behind as time goes by. Students like this cannot benefit from the many incidental opportunities for reading that surround them. They will do no pleasure reading. They will not be able to use reading in other subject areas. They fall farther and farther behind their higher-achieving peers and farther and farther behind their own potential.

The educational system should be duty bound to make certain that all students be assured success in the abundance mentioned in the Gospel according to Saint Matthew. Success for the students at risk for dropping out must be given. It must be structured into their curriculum. Success for these students is not something they can will themselves to do consciously. In our lock-step curricular structures, these students do not experience success. They are forced into the poor-get-poorer side of the cycle.

We unfortunately have a double standard in regard to success for our students (Forell, 1985). We provide high success, comfortable difficulty for high achievers, and little success with frustrating difficulty for low achievers. This double standard must be eliminated.

Students learn good work habits and have good attitudes toward work if they are given work that they can do. Students cannot learn good work habits when the work they are given is too difficult. They learn poor work habits, they develop negative attitudes toward work, and they learn to avoid work.

Success is not a panacea for the cure of individual differences in learning ability. The differences in ability will remain pronounced. However, the low achievers can benefit from the positive side of the Matthew effects. They should not become underachievers, curriculum casualties, and dropouts. The student that started with five gold talents

will still end up with ten, but now the student that started with one will
end up with two, not zero.

Specialization

Earlier in the chapter we spoke of the positive benefits of combining
curriculum-based assessment and cooperative learning arrangements. If
these are practiced, however, especially curriculum-based assessment,
teachers will find themselves in conflict with the specialized boundaries
of their grades or their content subject areas. The boundaries between
grades and subject areas are sharply drawn. Curriculum-based assessment requires that teachers identify each student's current instructional
level in any subject area and work with him or her at that level. We know
that the range of actual achievement of students in every grade and class
extends well below and above its designation. Because of the lock-step
curricular structure, teachers feel an obligation to their grade or content
subject area and level. They become curricular specialists for their
particular spot on the curricular path. This specialization causes additional problems. Teachers become proprietary about the curricular content assigned to their grade placement or content subject. They are
responsible for presenting a scope and sequence of content over each
academic year. This is presented with regard to the school calendar more
than with regard to student needs. The specialist system keeps the
curriculum assigned to grades and classes and not to students. The
specialist system needs drastic modification.

Systems that encourage specialists isolate teachers from responsibility to teach students. Their duty is to present the course content as
best they can. Their duty is to the curriculum content. They may work
very hard to present it as best they can, but it is too bad if some of the
students are not up to getting it. It is the teacher's duty to reach those
who can benefit.

Specialization encourages teachers to shift the responsibility for poor
performance and lack of achievement to others. If the student isn't
learning it is his fault. He should study harder. If students are not always
to blame for their own poor performance, then it was the poor performance of the teachers who preceded. They didn't get the student ready. It
may be the fault of the parents who don't discipline their children and
make them study more.

Teachers must become responsible for student achievement given where they are when they arrive at their classroom door. Some students will be functioning well below their grade-level assignment, some above it. Teachers need to find that level and start from there. This means that teachers must be well versed in the content and methods well below and well above their own place on the curriculum. Teachers of content subject areas must be prepared to deal with the curricular content that forms the readiness requirements of their courses. They must be prepared to teach it. All teachers should be grounded in curriculum-based assessment techniques and basic language arts methods.

At the secondary level some of the abuses of the specialist system are acute (Hargis, 1989). Legions of students march through specialists' rooms each day. One specialist alone may be responsible for teaching a particular subject and may have more than 150 different students in a day's time. Students pass in and out of these rooms in lock step. Those who don't remain in step drop out. Teachers deal with too many students to give much more attention than required to score tests for grades. Instruction is curriculum and teacher centered. Only about two minutes per week could possibly be devoted to in-class observation of students engaged in work. Teachers cannot become familiar with individual students.

Teachers should not see more than fifty students per day at the most. They should have the students over several subject areas daily and they should have the students for more than a year. Teachers should be obligated to teaching students where they are and for their ultimate achievement progress given the students' starting point when they first got them. At the elementary levels teachers should have students for several years, not just a single year (Wham, 1987).

The specialist system not only encourages shifting blame, it spawns the proliferation of still more specialists and special programs. Counselors and school psychologists are kept busy testing and classifying the problems of students who fail in the system. They then must find placements for the curriculum casualties in special programs that are really just safety-valve programs for the more troublesome students. The existence of such personnel and programs further reinforces the notion that the lock-step curriculum and the specialist system are fine. Unfortunately, for students who don't qualify for such services, there is no option available but to continue to fail or to drop out.

In summary, the lock-step curriculum and the specialist system are primary culprits in forcing a great many students to drop out. The abandonment of these systems together with the adoption of curriculum-based assessment methods and cooperative learning techniques are the recommended solutions.

Chapter 5

CURRICULUM CHANGES

A curriculum is the aggregate of the topics that make up the course of study in a school. The topics may require developmental presentations in reading, writing, and math. These individual courses of study are laid out in a skills hierarchy. In reading, writing, and math the scope and sequence of skills may cover eight or more school years. The content of other course work may be placed in the sequence according to their prerequisite readiness requirements. For example, a course in chemistry requires completion of a considerable amount of math and so will be placed in the curricular sequence after the necessary math topics. In the math curricula, subtraction and multiplication must be covered before long division. They are required subskills and are basic readiness requirements for long division.

The readiness relationship is not always so direct. Some curricular areas are fairly independent in terms of subject matter. However, most have at least a minimum level of reading ability as a fundamental readiness requirement. The curricular areas advance in difficulty and complexity as they include earlier learned skills. Though the particulars vary, the order and content for public school curricula are, in general, very similar.

The graded standardized curriculum emerged in mid-nineteenth century. Horace Mann was a leading proponent of it, along with the extension of public education to the secondary levels (McPherson, 1988). The curriculum structure that has evolved is superimposed on thirteen nine-month school years. This kindergarten through twelfth grade pattern is virtually standard in the United States.

We have been very critical of the problems our curricular organization causes at-risk students. The fact that students are grouped and assigned to the curriculum rather than the curriculum being assigned to individual students was a major point of criticism. The casualties caused by this lock-step organizational system, we feel, is the cause of the majority of our dropouts. Needless to say then, we feel that a primary reform move would be to break the lock-step pattern of curricular organization so as to permit students to move along at their own pace with maximum success.

The purpose of this chapter, however, is to suggest reforms to the content of the curriculum itself. One should always keep in mind, though, the problems which are induced by lock-step patterns even when content is changed. No matter how beneficial the things are that are being taught, they will not be learned if they are not presented at a level and pace that makes learning possible for individual students.

There are several forces currently affecting the nature of curriculum content in this country. All the forces want more rigor in the curriculum. All demand higher standards. One, usually designated as the "back-to-basics" movement, wants far more emphasis placed on the three R's. Another, feeling that America is losing its scientific, technical, and industrial leadership position in the world, wants more emphasis on science and math in the curriculum. Still others would have the curriculum emphasize "cultural literacy" or "great works."

These groups don't necessarily concur on the particulars of the curricular content, but they generally agree on the need for more demanding academic content. They typically want more academic content with more course work and more homework. They want higher standards, but they also want minimum standards.

Minimum competency tests or proficiency tests were developed to assure that students had what were judged to be minimum skills in reading, writing, and arithmetic. These tests were designed to make sure that students had attained the skill levels needed to pass these tests before they could be promoted or permitted to graduate from high school. School systems that developed such tests felt that no student should be permitted to graduate from high school without having attained this basal skill level. A high school diploma was supposed to mean something, and minimal competency testing was an attempt to make it so.

Minimal competency tests have had a novel effect on curriculum development. They have themselves formed the basis of curricula. When minimal competency testing is implemented, their importance becomes immediately apparent. Passing the test is a requirement for graduation. The test can be a substantial obstacle to graduation for many low-achieving students. In order to assure that students pass the test, teachers must make a concerted effort to teach to the test. The skills and content measured by the test forms the basis for curriculum development.

Some criticize the practice of developing a proficiency test curriculum.

Actually, it makes perfect pedagogical sense and it makes perfect measurement sense. Tests should be related to what is being taught. This teaching testing relationship is fundamental to good instruction and to test validity. Teachers should measure the effect of instruction and to do so they must have tests with high content validity. This is one of the fundamental principles of curriculum-based assessment which was outlined in the previous chapter, and it is the approach that we advocate. Testing and teaching must have this intimate relationship. Consequently, the relationship between curriculum and tests is as close to perfect as is possible.

The quality of a proficiency test-based curriculum can only be equal to the judgment of those responsible for constructing the test. This is true of the content of any curriculum. Proficiency tests typically have a basic skills orientation. Some might say they are watered-down versions of regular basic skills curricula. Regardless of their adjudged quality, they do offer a great opportunity for many students, particularly those who are mildly handicapped. The skill level of the items on proficiency tests are usually within the capacity level of a major portion of mildly handicapped students. Since many school systems make passing proficiency tests a requirement for graduation, this test makes it possible for students to get a regular diploma without going through the lock step of the regular curriculum. Getting a diploma, formerly impossible, becomes possible by going through a proficiency test-based curriculum.

Students in special classes or resource rooms can work at their own pace through the sequence of objectives which leads to passing the proficiency test. This can take an indeterminant length of time, depending on the ability of individual students. Since there is substantial intrinsic value in a high school diploma, a major, long-term effort can be devoted to the proficiency test curriculum. Some students at the margins of academic ability may take their entire school career to get there. We can only hope that the content of the proficiency test is good and useful; the effort required to pass it may be long term.

The GED test was intended for use with adults who have dropped out of school. However, it has been used for some time as an alternate route to a high school diploma for some mildly handicapped students who are unable to cope with the traditional lock-step curriculum. It has also formed the basis of high school curricula in prisons and other correctional facilities. Instruction focuses on passing the GED test. Again, this approach makes perfect sense in both practical and pedagogical terms. But, again, the content of the curriculum dictated by the GED test is criticized as being a watered-down basic skills curriculum.

The proficiency test and the GED test might be said to represent the basal academic curriculum. The highest levels of academic curricula might be said to represent the college prep curriculum. This takes different forms with advocates for an emphasis on great literary and cultural works, or advanced math and science. Those who advocate greater scope and rigor in the academic curriculum apparently feel that by simply including and demanding it of students that it will be learned.

We have tried to emphasize throughout the book that by holding a single standard for all students, casualties will inevitably result. We must come to terms with the fact that the normal range of achievement potential in each age group of students requires an entire range of academic curricular offerings to prevent such casualties. Further, we believe that there is too much in the curricula already in place. So much so, in fact, that it is impossible for most students to learn and retain it. Those who do learn it for a sufficient time to move through the curriculum successfully seldom retain the multitude of items in any useful form.

We believe that we should teach less in order to learn more. There should be far more careful consideration of what is important and utilitarian for students to learn. These are the items that should be included on the curriculum.

This is much more difficult than it sounds. In our society in this information age, we are overburdened with information. There are multitudes of things to teach which could be added to each curricular area moment-by-moment. At the same time, there are many competing notions as to what is important to learn. Suppose we consider math or science as an area in which we could reach a concensus as to what is critically important for every student to know. Even in these areas we find major disputes. We are just leaving the era in which the so-called new math dominated the curricular structure. We appear to be entering one that is more dominated by the back-to-the-basics movement. There has been an information explosion in science. Much new scientific information is added and becomes available constantly. At the same time, we have the continuing dispute over the creationist and evolutionist perspectives in biology.

The social studies curriculum is filling with information, a good deal of which can be considered controversial. The body of literature is expanding. If we included everyone's list of great books, we would have time for nothing else. Half of the list would be considered morally unsuitable by someone.

No more should be presented from an academic curriculum to any student than he or she can successfully learn and retain. In the current overloaded academic curricula, too much is presented; consequently less can be learned. If less is presented with adequate provision for meaningful drill and repetition, far more will be learned. Critics of American education often are critical of student performance on specific tests. Students seem to have glaring deficiencies in areas that would seem to be common wisdom. They are critical of our performance on these same tests relative to students in other countries. We believe that the critics would have much less opportunity to condemn if our curricula were focused on areas of common wisdom or were as concentrated on narrow subject areas as those of students in other countries.

Nevertheless, for the purposes of dealing with students at risk for dropping out, the academic curricular content should be limited to the capacity of individual students. This may fall anywhere between the proficiency test level to the college prep level.

We have developed an idealized image of what students should learn. It is an academic and scholarly image. It is based on a curriculum full of rigor. There are a number of views concerning the particular makeup of this curriculum, but all views emphasize math, science, great literature, and history. These curricula are probably quite appropriate for those students who are able to benefit from them, but we must remember that we can't make all students scholars simply by trying to force them into that mold. We may have the objective of "cultural literacy" but find that we have produced instead social incompetence. In the process of forcing students into such curricular molds, we produce casualties. We must learn to consider each student's individual ability level. We must learn to honor achievement to potential as much as we honor achievement to the standard imposed by some curriculum. We must structure success into the core objectives of all curriculum and methods. We cannot do this by requiring the same thing for all students.

Not all students are, or should be, going to college, and not nearly as many students should be failing and dropping out of school. This means that we must permit students to work at many different levels. Schools also need to attend to more basic objectives. Curricular content needs to attend to helping students function as citizens.

We need to change the curriculum to include objectives that help students stay healthy, out of jail, and employed. Our current lack of curricular attention to these objectives permits many pushouts and curriculum casualties to become societal burdens.

One of the authors (Hargis, 1989) has described an idealized high school curriculum which deals with both academic and life skill curricula. He developed the idea as a humane alternative to a highly academic college prep curriculum proposed by a recent Secretary of the Department of Education. The secretary proposed the James Madison High School Curriculum. The Hargis curriculum posed for students who are at risk for dropping out was for the hypothetical Emiliano Zapata High School.

The curriculum of Zapata High is designed to respect individual differences. It structures-in success and honors normally unappreciated accomplishments such as being able to live independently without being a burden on society. It has baseline objectives for all its students. They are contained in its curriculum which is called the healthy, out-of-jail, and employed curriculum, the HOJE curriculum.

Zapata has a very different type of curriculum perspective than that of Madison. At Madison, the curricular objectives are set well above the basal ability level of most students. There, the perspective is that students should reach up, be challenged, achieve high academic objectives. Only in reaching and straining can these objectives be attained. You must have high expectations for all students. Slower students especially should be challenged.

At Zapata High, success is fundamental and the curriculum is so ordered. The challenge called for really means a double standard will be applied. It honors with prominent curricular emphasis the basic life skills that students need to be independent citizens. The curriculum must have these as the basal objectives so that low-achieving students can succeed as do their counterparts who are high achievers. This does not mean that the Zapata curriculum is only HOJE. This is just the basal or minimum expectation for all students. If the HOJE objectives are all that a particular low achiever can attain, that is just fine. This would be considered an excellent and honorable accomplishment. Remember though, this is a basal objective. All students who have the ability will work toward the same academic goals that the Madison High students do. The difference between the schools is that Zapata attends to individual differences and students can work along a curriculum ladder at a pace that permits success. It fully expects students to come out with many different skills or academic levels. However, it expects that all students will leave with HOJE skills at a minimum.

Madison High has only the top academic objectives to work toward. It will produce many casualties. Naturally, the top academic students will survive. The school is designed for them. The lower-achieving students will drop out or, if they survive at all, will have no independent living skills.

Even without a life-skill dimension to a curriculum, just the attainment of a diploma has utility in and of itself. Consequently, even if the curriculum is academic rather than life skill-oriented, it should be paced to individual needs. Failure is non-productive. Students do not willingly fail. If students fail, they can't achieve to their personal potential. Success must dominate the curricular assignment to students of all achievement levels. Students must be placed at a level on either type of curriculum where they can succeed. They must be maintained at their appropriate instructional level.

The curriculum at Zapata High is flexible. Students can emphasize a life-skill curriculum or an academic one. The curriculum may be a combination of the two, depending on the needs of individual students. The emphasis may be more or less in either direction. Also, life skills will be integrated in academic subjects wherever possible and the academic subjects will be integrated in the life skills. The curriculum will be assigned and fitted to students. It will not be assigned to grades and courses.

The teachers at Zapata High are prepared to teach students with the wide range of normal ability levels. All teachers can teach any of the basic academic subject areas in addition to a specialty where they may be a resource person. This permits the integration of the HOJE curriculum, the proficiency test curriculum, and the college prep curriculum.

Course work is not compartmentalized at Zapata as it is at Madison or for that matter in any conventional curriculum organization. All teachers at Zapata feel the obligation to attend to all basic curricular areas. This includes a considerable range of difficulty levels in each area. All of the teachers know that they must work with each student at whatever level he or she has attained when arriving at their room.

An activity of primary importance to Zapata High is teachers determining where instruction should start with each student in any of the subject areas. A student's current instructional level in regard to the readiness requirements of the subject must be determined for each student. The scope and sequence of skills which makes up each curricular area should be used as a checklist to determine with accuracy where a student is. This is the place where instruction should commence. It is the student's entry or readiness level.

The typical school curriculum isolates students. They are placed in isolated, competitive relationships by the lock-step order and the grading practices. Resnick (1987) makes a stark and contrasting comparison between the way learning is organized in school and in situations out of school. She notes that the dominant form of learning in school is individual. She notes that for the most part a student succeeds or fails independently of what other students do unless affected by normative grading practices. However, in contrast, learning activity outside of school is socially shared. The ability to function successfully is dependent on what others do and how the performance of other persons in the social context mesh. The curriculum at Zapata High is conducted in supportive social contexts.

The curriculum is structured to resemble the learning activities that go on outside school. Journeyman apprentice relationships and shared work are built into the supervised study, peer tutoring, and cooperative learning groups that are fundamental parts of the instructional delivery system at Zapata. Social skill development is a primarily important curricular item in the HOJE curriculum. Cooperative learning activities are intrinsically social in nature, and foster social skill development. However, social skills are only acquired by long-term participation in healthy social activities. The social learning activities are both a vehicle for advancing learning and the thing to be learned.

The isolating, competitive, lock-step curricula, together with the grading systems that perpetuate them, fail in regard to learning and possibly even worse: they foster the development of asocial or antisocial behaviors in students who cannot compete well within them. These curricula not only fail students and cause many to drop out, they also put them at risk to be failures in life outside school. .

How can conventional curriculum topics be handled in a system that uses curriculum-based assessment, uses cooperative learning techniques, and insists on success? How could it be managed in a subject such as literature? It is a fact that the standard literature anthologies in use typically are comprised of selections with readability levels more difficult than those possessed by the lower-achieving members of the classes using them. Readability of the selection is the primary concern. Students cannot understand, let alone enjoy or appreciate, literary works that exceed their reading skill level. Readable literature is what is needed in order to produce these benefits. No student learns to enjoy or appreciate literature unless their exposure to it comes with enjoyment and success.

Requiring a student with a sixth grade reading skill to read Shakespeare's plays will insure that the student hates them. No appreciation for reading or for literature comes by forcing students into books that they have neither the skill nor the background experience to understand.

Literature anthologies or readings selected for literature classes should be evaluated on readability. Books and selections of literary quality do vary greatly in reading difficulty. The readability level of the selection should match the reading skill of individual students.

We do not suggest that literary works should be abridged or watered down so that they can be understood. We believe that purpose of literature in the curriculum should be honored in spirit and to the letter. However, this means that readable and relevant literature must be identified for a variety of skill levels. Imposing a list of "great" works or a standard anthology on these students meets neither the letter nor the spirit. It usually just makes at-risk students hate the subject.

A curricular area that is often loaded with overwhelming numbers of details is the social studies. The vast number of facts: names, dates, places, and events are neither meaningful, nor learnable for low-achieving students. However, there are important things to learn from social studies. The legal and social structure of the community where students live is important information to have knowledge of in order to live and survive. Keeping on the right side of the law should not be a matter left to chance. The social studies curriculum should attend to this issue specifically.

The cooperative social structure emphasized at Zapata High, in the curriculum and in the instructional delivery system, is designed to help the students learn to live peacefully and helpfully in society. Learning to be an acceptable citizen may be an extra long-term effort. It may take awhile for many students to learn that "one's freedom ends where one's neighbor's nose begins."

The citizenship model provided at school may have to suffice for many students. Respect and consideration of others must be demonstrated by the school toward the student. This is shown in convincing fashion when the school does no violence to the students through the use of grading systems. Low-achieving students need no additional reminders of their level of achievement relative to other students. The teachers at Zapata very carefully identify where the students can work effectively and see that they work there successfully. Students learn that teachers want them to work well and successfully, and that failure, simply for being less able, is not a possible consequence in this humane and supportive environment. Every student is to do as well as he or she can do. Every student is encouraged to, and feels obligated to, help other students. Indeed, this is the social learning component of the curriculum.

Geography is also a part of social studies and it should first be related to where the student lives. Many students will have had very restricted experiences. The instruction must, nevertheless, be made meaningful. All of the students must learn their area geography and transportation systems in sufficient detail to deal with persisting life problems, and to open employment opportunities that might otherwise be ignored. Presently, a great deal of time is devoted to the study of geography without ever attending to these basic life needs. Such information is neither learnable nor utilitarian for low achievers.

What and how much history should be taught? Certainly the study of history is important. Humans have an enormous propensity for repeating mistakes. We will not make judgments about the specific curricular content. However, there is a fundamental consideration regardless of what is included in the history curriculum. Do not include more for any given student than he or she can learn successfully. We have a powerful tendency to cram everything in - not to overlook anything that might be important. When we overwhelm students with content, they will learn almost nothing. The students themselves should demonstrate how much and how far they should go in any subject. Some students will have a considerable interest in and capacity to learn a variety of academic subjects including history. At Zapata High, students are neither overwhelmed nor limited by a rigid curriculum.

How much science should be included? Again, this is subject to the individual differences of the students. Certainly the most important things have utility. Science should be related to health and nutrition, safety and the myriad of science-related problems encountered in daily living. We live in a chemical, electronic, and mechanical environment of almost overwhelming complexity. The curriculum for the low-achieving students should include, first of all, those elements of science that will assist them in living safely and healthily within it.

The curriculum devoted to health, physical education and recreation is important at Zapata High. But it is a grand departure from the typical curriculum in this area. Far less time is devoted to conventional sports. Non-competitive activities that emphasize health and fitness dominate the curriculum. As Roberts (cited in Kutner, 1989) points out, between the ages of twelve and sixteen about 80 to 90 percent of students drop out of organized sports, especially the highly competitive ones. The same pattern appears among teenagers who drop out of music when they have participated in music competitions. Children who drop out of sports do so because of the emphasis on winning claims D. L. Feltz (cited in Kutner, 1989). Traditional curricula emphasize competition. The curriculum should be devoted to playing as a social activity without grading performance or keeping scores.

Students need the opportunity to engage in physical activity that permits them to feel success and acquire a feeling of competence. Tumbling and gymnastics offers much opportunity for both. Aerobic exercise such as jumping rope, aerobic dancing, or running can give the student a sense of success and accomplishment through simple participation. These can also be a boon to students with weight and appearance problems. How a student manages liesure-time is critically important. The curriculum should make sure that it finds activities and outlets for students that keep them out of trouble. There are multitudes of innocent ways to blunder into trouble. Students need to learn acceptable recreational activities that will fully engage their leisure time while they are in school and during life thereafter.

We do not mean to suggest that competitive activities are altogether inappropriate. They are appropriate for students who are competitive and relish competition. Remember, however, competitive sports and recreational activities are not appropriate for most students. They are only something else to avoid or drop out of.

Students need to learn to engage their time fully and productively. Organizing their time around part-time jobs can help students get job experience and learn work-related skills. Zapata High encourages employment of students. It attempts to facilitate a work-study relationship to help students be better employees and to manage their finances. Much of the curriculum can be made more meaningful and relevant by encouraging the development of work-study programs with local employers.

Vocational and career education grow naturally from the work-study program. This area of the curriculum needs to emphasize basic economic independence. Community resources provide the basic training centers wherever possible. The transition from school to work need not be abrupt.

The curriculum at Zapata High honors achievement at all levels, from the basic HOJE level to the highly academic. It respects the need of all students to experience success and accomplishment at any level. By respecting the students and providing a secure and humane environment for them, respect is given in return.

Chapter 6

SUMMING UP

I am afraid that little has changed to improve the lot of at-risk students since the publication of the first edition of *Dropouts*. The lock-step curriculum still has a stranglehold on our nation's school organization, and our system of grades and grading still affirms its continuance.

There are some bright spots, however. Whether or not these can provide enough illumination to help lead us away from our old ways of thinking is still an uncertainty.

In one of the northwestern states there is movement to abandon grades for more useful and substantive means of noting achievement progress. Unfortunately, in others, there is an indication that the use of grades will be emphasized and in more punitive ways. For the most part, grades remain a firm part of our mental makeup and attitude. Grades are still mistakenly equated with standards and harsh grading with high standards.

Reform is constantly discussed, but the terms of discussion reveal our lock-step view of our educational system. When we speak of reforms, we talk of changes and standards for the grades K through 12. We seldom think of reforming this organization system itself. This organizational structure, K through 12, is an essential part of the problem in dealing with at-risk students.

I have heard of one novel program which appears to effectively nullify some of the evils of the lock-step. This program is called "Running Start." It is a program for high achieving students that, if modified, could serve low achieving, at-risk students also.

I heard about the program in an interview of a high-school senior who had been in a running start program in her school. The program she described permitted academically able students to obtain college level credit for approved course work taken during the junior and senior year in high school. By the time of graduation, she would have enough college credit to give her junior standing in the college she was planning on attending.

It certainly is possible for high achieving students to compress the amount of time it takes to complete a public school curriculum. There is no reason to squelch the achievement progress of academically able students by making them conform to the lock-step.

Harper Lee vividly illustrates this problem in *To Kill a Mocking Bird.* When 6-year-old Jean Louise started first grade her teacher, Miss Caroline, was quite upset by the child's precocious reading proficiency. Jean Louise read everything on the chalkboard, most of the first reader, and the stock market quotations from the *Mobile Register.* Miss Caroline, being quite irritated by this demonstration, told Jean Louise to tell her father to stop teaching her. It would interfere with her learning to read in school.

Also, however, in Jean Louise's classroom were children without the skill or even the readiness that she had. Some were even repeating the first grade. Rather than repeating a lock-step grade cycle, progress could and should be made in a continuous fashion: the curriculum content of the first grade might be completed by adding a few months. Children should be able to build on whatever progress they have made without having to start entirely over at the beginning of the grade cycle. Time at each stage of skill development should be no more or no less than the individual child needs.

Some students can finish the curriculum given more time. Why not let some students take an additional year or more to complete the curriculum? Why should we fail a student in a course like algebra because he can't keep up. He might do well in the course if it provided the extra necessary time and practice to reach the necessary level of proficiency. Failure to keep pace in the lock-step is a principal cause of failing grades and of non-achievement. The duration of grade levels and of courses should be sufficiently flexible or open-ended to permit students to attain curricular objectives. Our aim for all students should be the attainment of the skill, not the length of time it takes to reach it. The educational destination is the important thing. Many students do not and will not arrive at the desired destination if the time to reach it is held constant for all students.

Grades, if this form of school organization is retained at all, should permit students to pass through at their own instructional rate. Some students could compress and master the content of a grade in much less than nine months. Others would require considerably more than the nine months allotted to the grade. Curricular content should not be assigned to fixed time periods.

With the present lock-step organization, students who might have benefitted from an additional few months of time to master course content find themselves failing and are required to complete the entire nine month grade. This is terribly inefficient. On the other hand, students who could have covered more advanced content in that time are constrained and so achieve less than they could.

Of course, making these changes requires a different model of teaching and classroom organization. It means that the teacher cannot be concerned with presenting the prescribed and proscribed content over each of the 180 school days. Students must be guided through learning on the curricular path, and the curricular content must be made accessible to each student at a level and rate at which he or she can learn most efficiently.

We have become so limited in vision that we view our standards from the lock-step perspective. When we set standards for students we do so from the lock-step, grade level viewpoint. This has unfortunate consequences. The standards are the same for all students, and the standards are assigned to grades not to students. Useful standards can only be determined by assessment. Determining the individual student's current achievement level on the curricular sequence is the first and necessary step in determining useful standards. Our standard should be to successfully achieve the next level of competence in the most efficient way.

Assigning standards to grades often causes us to overlook where students are on a curriculum when they arrive at any given grade. On average, the actual achievement level for 50 percent of the students entering any grade will be different than the level for the grade. Having the same grade-assigned standard for all students entering each grade will suppress achievement for those students functioning above their grade level and will severely limit the achievement of those students who enter the grade with skills below it.

There is much ranting and raving from educational critics as well as from the educational establishment that we must have high standards for our students; our problem, they claim, is that we expect too little. Despite the volume of the ranting, it should be made clear to those who hold this view that our standards are inappropriate if they are out of reach for some and at the same time set too low for others.

Many children are receiving failing grades simply because the standard of the grade level is out of their reach. It is also ironic that teachers who feel they have high standards are hard graders. They artificially place the attainment of good grades so high that relatively few students can attain them. They forget that learning is the standard we should be seeking, not a grade, and that successful learning and therefore doing well is the standard we should hold for all.

I have attempted to describe and to illustrate the extent to which children fit the lock-step organization of our grades and curriculum. Since the publication of the first edition of this book, this author rediscovered a graphic illustration from Lawrence W. Carrillo's little book, *Informal Reading-Readiness Experiences* (1964). This graphic, published one generation ago, still accurately reflects the range of individual differences that exist in classrooms in grades one through eight. Its accuracy can be confirmed by examining the normative data from popularly-used reading achievement tests in current use. Carrillo's chart (Figure 2) is reproduced here to provide a more concrete illustration of how well children fit the Procrustean bed of our lock-step school organization.

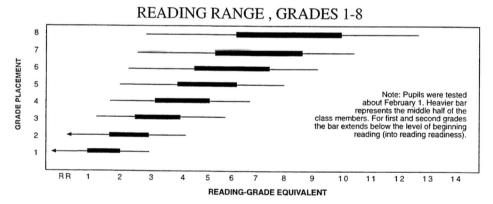

Figure 2. Carillo, Lawrence W., (1964) *Informal Reading-Readiness Experience*. San Francisco: Chandler Publishing Co.

Part 2

A Human Service Perspective

Chapter 7

RELATED LITERATURE

Dropping out is not an isolated phenomenon. Dropouts cut across many strata of American people and the agencies that deal with them, including welfare, mental health, corrections, and education. If education could effectively deal with these students, welfare, mental health, and correctional systems would not have to. Appropriate intervention at the school level must include research that clearly defines the dropout, determines the path that the dropout follows in leaving school, and establishes an intervention that is based on these findings.

Literature to date includes topics ranging from the difficulty of definition to the lack of ability to compete in the labor force. Hahn (1987) states that high dropout rates threaten the nation's productivity and represent a terrible waste of young lives. This, of course, is not that far removed from James B. Conant's warning that the dropout problem is social dynamite (1961). Hahn (1987) further elaborates on the problem of definitions of dropouts by stating

> Most social initiatives build on a foundation of accurate viable data. When we attempt to address the problems and needs of potential and actual dropouts much of the essential data are lacking.
> We have informed *estimates* [emphasis ours] of how many students nationally are dropping out, of how many are poor, are members of minority groups and of how many are doing well or poorly in school. But on the level that really counts—in local districts and individual schools—we simply don't know.

This makes comparison across districts virtually impossible.

The problem with the definition of dropouts is one that is endemic to social science: that of matching indicators to concepts. There is always a shadow that falls between the two. In other words, there is seldom a perfect match between concepts and indicators. Here is the definition provided by the Department of Education:

A dropout is a student who:

1. was enrolled in the district at some time during the previous school year
2. was not enrolled at the beginning of the current regular school year
3. has not graduated or completed a program of studies by the maximum age established by the State
4. has not transferred to another public school district, or to a non-public school, or to a state-approved education program
5. has not left school because of illness or school-approved absence. (Federal Register, 1988)

This definition implies that dropouts will be determined on a yearly basis. With a longitudinal data base, the rate may also be computed by subtracting the number of graduating seniors from the number of freshmen enrolled four years earlier; taking into consideration points 3, 4, and 5 listed above.

Correlates of Dropping Out

"Dropping out is a problem not confined to a handful of minority students who couldn't learn" (Hahn, 1987).

The Government Employment Office reported that in 1985, 4.3 million young people between the ages of 16 and 24 dropped out of school — 13 percent of that age group. Of these, 3.5 million were white, 700,000 were black, and 100,000 were from other groups. Moreover, male dropouts outnumbered female dropouts. Approximately 16 percent of males between the ages of 18 and 19 were dropouts, while only 12 percent of females in the same ages group had dropped out (Hahn, 1987). Significant factors that have been associated with leaving school include socioeconomic status, attendance at school, involvement in school activities, academic achievement, ability to read, social skills, race, gender, and appropriate age for grade.

Kaplan and Luck (1977) found that as many as 50 percent of the dropouts had been held back at least once. And Schreiber (1964) estimated that a student who failed first or second grade had an 80 percent chance of dropping out (Larsen & Shertzer, 1987). Sewell et al. (1981) suggest that factors other than intelligence are at work in explaining grade failure, grade retention, and dropping out. Moos (1970) and Kronick (1972) recommend the investigation of ecological variables including home life and the social climate of the school. Hargis (1987) strongly recommended the use of a curriculum tailored to the individual child which he terms curriculum-based assessment. Hargis believed that what we have are curriculum casualties rather than children with learning disabilities or conduct disorders.

Regarding the dropout's family, Rumberger (1983) and Cervantes (1965) posited that a good predictor of dropping out would be the child's parent's not graduating from high school. The common wisdom also predicts that the majority of dropouts will come from lower socio-economic status homes (Bachman, 1972; Elliott et al., 1967; Sewell et al., 1981).

School attendance has been found to be a good predictor of dropping out. Non-attendance in elementary school shows a moderate correlation with non-attendance in high school and eventually dropping out. That child who regularly attended elementary school but who begins to miss in high school is a very different person than the child who was absent in the elementary school before entering high school. The latter child is much more likely to be involved with alcohol and/or drugs than the former child.

Involvement in school activities is another predictor of not staying in school. Belonging to a social club, athletic team, or academic honor society is predicted to be a hedge against dropping out.

Race is another variable that tends to be correlated with dropping out. The findings here are probably confounded by the effects of socioeconomic status. Many studies report that, proportionally, American Indians and Hispanics have the highest dropout rate, followed by Blacks, Whites, and Asians (Kunisawa, 1987).

Because dropouts do not take part in school organizations and do not acquire and hold summer jobs, they lack many important social skills. This lack of social skill development also appears in another group that drops out: the gifted.

A final predictor of dropping out is region of the country. Mixed findings have been reported here. This is interesting, in that one would think that at least there would be agreement on where the dropout rate is the highest. These mixed findings confirm the quagmire that exists in the study and implementations of interventions for dropouts.

Are students in certain parts of the country at greater risk of dropping out? Hahn (1987) found notable self-reported differences both by region and size of city. The states in the Southwest suffered the highest dropout rate (21%), while the rate stood at 18 percent for the Northeast, at 11 percent in the Southeast, and 9 percent in the Northwest. Dropout rates were the lowest in the Midwest (Hahn, 1987).

Data gathered during the same year and reported in another study by Kunisawa (1987) showed the following states with the highest dropout percentages: (1) Louisiana, 43.7; (2) Alabama, 37.9; (3) Florida, 37.8; (4) New York, 37.8; (5) Mississippi, 37.6; (6) Georgia, 36.9; (7) California, 36.8; (8) South Carolina, 35.5; (9) Arizona, 35.4; and (10) Texas, 35.4.

Outcomes of Dropping Out

A number of outcomes have been associated with dropping out of school. These include high unemployment, a high incidence of health problems, increasing needs for welfare assistance, an increase in mental health problems and high crime and delinquency rates (Catterall, 1986; Lanier, 1986). Jones (1977) found that the unemployed dropout was six to ten times more likely to be involved in criminal activities than is an employed individual. Kronick, in working with the Community Alternatives to Prison project in Knoxville, Tennessee, has found the typical applicant to the project to be male, white, 25, an alcohol and/or drug abuser, able to read on a third grade level, and one who quit school in the ninth grade.

Keeping children in school must be seen as a cost-effective way of keeping them as adults out of correction, mental health, and welfare programs.

SUMMARY DISCUSSION

What can one say about dropouts up to this point? First, there is a problem with definition, data collection, and analysis, and hence group comparison. Without a clear-cut definition of the problem, there cannot be quality intervention or true awareness of how great the problem is. Some school districts have inclusive, while other districts have exclusive definitions of dropouts. The results are either inflated or depressed figures. One district might want to report a high dropout rate in order to secure state or federal grants, while another district might want to underreport its dropout figures in order not to look bad and at the same time give the impression that they have a model system.

Interventions on dropouts must be based on reliable and valid data, and hence this basic and beginning point must be addressed. The definition cited earlier of using twelfth grade graduates, subtracted from the ninth grade class of four years earlier, seems effective, assuming random in-and-out migration and taking into consideration death, early graduation, late graduation, transfer to vocational or other special schools, etc.

Once basic agreement on what constitutes a dropout is established, interventions can be planned and executed. In this text, one of the central interventions that will be stressed is that of curriculum-based assessment developed by Hargis (1987). This individualized instruction method, where the curriculum, rather than the student, is changed, is discussed in detail in Chapter 4.

One mode of attack on the problem of dropouts is to look at the characteristics that differentiate dropouts from graduates.

The following characteristics have been discussed by various authors as critical in examining dropouts.

The Person

1. Academic Ability

   Dropouts have been found to have lower IQs than graduates, to be behind in reading and math, and to be lacking in general academic skills.
2. Age

   Dropouts tend to be held back in their schooling and to be one or two years older than their peers.
3. Socioeconomic Status

   Dropouts tend to come from lower socioeconomic status backgrounds than graduates.
4. Race

   Dropouts tend to come from non-white, rather than white, racial backgrounds. One study reported earlier ranked dropouts in descending order as American Indian, Hispanic, Black, White, and Asian.
5. Gender

   Males tend to drop out more often than females and for different but possibly related reasons. Males often report dropping out for financial reasons, either to help out at home or to support a family, while females report dropping out to start a home or because of pregnancy.

6. Family Background

   It is reported that dropouts tend to come from families in which parents are not graduates. It is also reported that homes where mothers create an environment where studying can be done have fewer dropouts than homes where this environment is not created.

7. Locus of Control

   The concept of personal control stems from the work of Julian Rotter (1975). According to Rotter, a control orientation refers to the extent to which an individual perceives an event as occurring as a result of his/her own actions, which he termed internal control, or whether the individual has the belief that events have a luck, chance, or fortuitous base, which Rotter labelled external control. Most research reports that dropouts report external rather than internal locus of control.

8. School Social Activities

   Dropouts tend not to be a part of social activities or clubs within schools. They report not being members of athletic teams, social clubs, the band, the photography club, or an honor society. Many socialization skills that are learned in school are not learned by the dropout. Many dropouts lose jobs because of this lack of basic social skills.

9. Peer Group

   Research by Elliott and Voss (1974) reflect that dropouts may be affected by differential association and normlessness within the school. If the at-risk youth associates with other at-risk youths or dropouts, the probability is high that he or she will drop out because of the differential association factor. Differential association was defined by Sutherland (1947) as ways in which criminal behavior was learned. He stressed that criminal behavior was learned in the same way that normative behavior was learned: in small intimate groups. This learning included techniques of behavior, as well as the learning of definitions as favorable or unfavorable toward crime. Since dropping out may be a group phenomenon, what Glueck and Glueck (1968) referred to as the "flock phenomenon," group counseling may not be a good intervention to use. This will be discussed later in the text.

10. Self-Concept

    The common wisdom is that dropouts will have lower self-concepts than graduates. However, it has been reported that some dropouts, especially Hispanics, experience a rise in self-concept when they leave the school. This suggests the validity of strain theory, that the school provides no opportunity for positive status attainment, but that the home and neighborhood do. Strain theory claims that deviant behavior is a result of the malintegration of cultural ends and societal means (Merton, 1957).

The above ten concepts describe students at risk and would focus the point of intervention on the individual. However, some researchers, especially Wehlage (1986), claim the point of concern should be the school. He claims that research needs to focus on the characteristics of the school rather than that of the student. Most students do not report seeing themselves dropping out earlier in their schooling. In asking high school sophomores, it appears that as they look back on their school years, they did not see leaving school as something that they planned or would eventually do. Yet, what appears continually in the literature is that the dropout reports "School was not for me" as the main reason for leaving. Hence, something within the very nature of the school is operating to facilitate these youth in their leaving school. This phenomenon is often referred to as pushout rather than dropout.

Yesseldyke (1988) stated that there are three key factors that lead to a student being placed in special education: (1) teacher squeak, (2) student characteristics, and (3) available resources. Considering the first, if the teacher wants the student out of the classroom badly enough, the student is gone. It might well be that this same process works for pushing students out of school instead of into special education classes.

If meaningful insights into the problems of the dropout are to be achieved, issues which are centered around the impact of the educational system should be further explored. Institutional deficiencies have been given significantly less attention than individual factors (Sewell et al., 1981). To pay more attention to the institution as opposed to the individ ual allows for greater insight into at-risk students but makes the problem much more difficult to deal with. At the same time, focusing on the school removes the blaming of the victim ideology that is so deeply ingrained in American society. The school should be held accountable for its role in the failure of at-risk students.

Earlier theoretical work (Rokeach, 1960; Moos, 1970; Halpin & Croft, 1963) has developed concepts such as open or closed climates to describe personality types or social organizations such as prisons, psychiatric hospitals, and schools. The term open was defined as basically allowing individual freedom and flexibility, a closed climate as basically inflexible and allowing little freedom in behavior. Moos developed the social climate scale that could be used to determine perceived organizational press by members of the organization. Kronick (1972) adapted the Moos scale to a school setting. The basic premise from an organizational perspective was that demographically high-risk students—male, black, low socioeconomic status, low IQ—who perceived the climate as open, would have higher grades than female, white, high socioeconomic status, high IQ students who perceived the school climate as closed. Though the numbers were small, the hypothesis was supported with explained variance approaching 50 percent.

Other than the school might be perceived as open or closed, or that certain climate dimensions, such as perceived autonomy, support, involvement, and insight, are related to student behavior, what else can be said about the school that pushes students out? The hypothesis here is that closed school climates will be more likely to push a student out of school than an open climate will.

The emphasis in dropout research so far has focused far more on the student than the school. Research on the school as an organization has been described by Stinchcombe (1964), Barker and Gump (1964), and Halpin and Croft (1963).

> The major conclusion is that rebellious behavior is largely a reaction to the school itself and to its promises, not a failure of the family or community. High school students can be motivated to conform by paying them in the realistic coin of future adult advantages. Except perhaps for pathological cases, any student can be made to conform if the school can realistically promise something valuable to him or her as a reward for working hard. But for a large part of the population, especially the adolescents who will enter the male working class or the female candidates for early marriage, the school has nothing to promise. (Stinchcombe, 1964)

Finally, the issue of student school interaction must be taken into account when attempting to understand dropout behavior. As Mann (1986) reported, the way young people experience school is the most frequently given reason for leaving school early. Sewell et al. (1981) also found that the educational policies and practices of schools which may have contributed in subtle and unintentional ways to the perception of low socioeconomic status children that schooling will not extricate them from positions of powerlessness nor will it enhance their aspirations for economic and social mobility.

ORGANIZATIONAL EFFECTS—THE SCHOOL

In studying organizational effects on human behavior the works of Goffman (1961), Cressey (1961), and Rosenhahn (1973) are followed. Is an individual's response affected more by one of his or her own traits or more by perceptions of the situation? The following quote from Donald Cressey is relevant here:

Many traits exhibited by individual inmates or staff members in a correctional organization may well be the result of properties of the organization rather than of the person and that diagnosis and explanation of personality disorders and other deviant behavior must show concern for the organizational context in which behavior occurs. (P. 50)

The relevance of Cressey's material to schools is that students, staff, and faculty may well act in accordance with perceived organizational expectations of the school rather than on their own desired interests.

According to Warner and DeFleur (1969), the behavioral setting is either of high or of low social constraint. A setting of high social constraint is one in which the individual's behavior takes place under conditions where it is likely that others will be aware of it. The author's assumption is that the school sets an environment of high social constraint and hence elicits desired responses and molds behavior as it, the school, so desires. What becomes of interest to us at this point is what then are the behaviors that the school in America wants today. As Moos (1970) states, the press of the environment as the student perceives it establishes the direction behavior should take if one is to find satisfaction within the school. From our perspective, it is hoped that the school would operate with high constraint that would support student learning and at the same time make an environment to overcome the negative attitudes that the student might bring to the school.

Contemporary evidence suggests that schools are in many ways operating in a fashion that is counterproductive to learning. Schools today work on competitive rather than cooperative models where some students must lose and eventually fail. Another inference regarding student behavior is that the school appears to reward compliant or even submissive behavior and to punish individual non-compliant, or even creative behavior.

Earlier research by Kronick (1972) found that on the Moos scale, autonomy and spontaneity were low for eighth grade respondents and that they saw themselves as having minimal control over their environment. In regards to the submission and autonomy scales, results report the student adapting to a submissive role within the school. This study, which included some unstructured interviews, found that students felt that they were adapting to the organization's rules and acting in a non-genuine way in order to get along in school. Specific rules, such as dress codes, no running when late for class, and girls and boys not being allowed to hold hands, seemed to the students to be counterproductive to their well-being and strictly for the convenience of the school.

In regards to the importance of the characteristics of schools and how children learn, landmark research by Coleman et al. (1966) found very little to support the relationship between what educators deem important and achievement in school, by which he meant grades. They found that minority children were more sensitive to school characteristics than whites. To emphatically illustrate this point, Coleman states "The relatively small amount of variation in achievement that school characteristics (as compared to the student's background) account for depends much more on the people at the school—other students and teachers—than on facilities and curricula" (Coleman, 1966). The Coleman report focused on physical plant in looking at organizational effects, whereas the present authors focus on the entire ecological structure of the school including neighborhood, physical plant and facilities, curricula offered, faculty, staff and students. Coleman further found two student attitudes that were highly correlated with academic achievement but not related to school characteristics according to their findings. These were: self-concept and sense of control over the environment. These two factors are directly related to Moos's concept of organizational climate and would appear to be related to characteristics of the school, though this is denied in Coleman's research. Coleman found that self-concept and control over the environment accounted for more variation in achievement than family background or school characteristics by which Coleman meant physical plant. It would appear that control over the environment is reflected in the autonomy, spontaneity, and submission dimensions of the organizational climate outlined by Moos (1970) and that self-concept is a reflection of the degree to which these dimensions are attained.

These findings suggest that the school can overcome negative student characteristics in dealing with academic achievement.

As mentioned earlier, schools appear to follow a competitive rather than a cooperative model where some students must ultimately lose. The question "What would happen if everyone succeeded in school?" is one that must throw terror into the hearts and minds of many educators. Discussion of this issue is an important point for this book. Talcott Parsons (1965), in describing a public school classroom, put it this way:

> One way of describing the present pattern in its moral aspects is to say that it is fundamentally individualistic. It tends to maximize the desirability of autonomy and responsibility in the individual. Yet this is an institutionalized individualism in that it is mostly controlled at the moral level. The achievement and the success of the individual must ideally be in accord with the rules above all with those which guarantee opportunity to all and which keep the system in line with its remoter values.

In the interest of effectiveness, personal achievement must often be in the context of the collective organization, thus further limiting individual autonomy. Personal autonomy is systematically disallowed and the individual is not permitted to reach his/her potential in the school.

In American society, where achievement is revered and where new standards are rising in the school, different sectors of American society have historically responded in far different fashion to the demands of higher education. In the 1960s, Parsons noted: "In the case of the school there is a markedly greater acceptance of the evaluation of good work and its importance for the future." This trend, however, has not held for those of the lower sector of American society. The increased pressure from the school to do well has been met by the middle class in a positive way, but the lower class has tended to respond in a deviant rather than in a conformative way. Increased educational expectations have put an increased pressure on those who are disadvantaged. As mentioned earlier with the emphasis placed on achievement, those who cannot keep up will fall by the wayside, some quietly, some not so quietly. We will "flag" those who leave school through the route of expulsion for unacceptable behavior. They will have come to the awareness of agents of social control, whether they be guidance counselors, juvenile officers, or the police. But what about the child who quietly slips off unnoticed by school or other personnel? Are they different—qualitatively, quantitatively? These students are leaving school because they too don't measure up to the standards of achievement extant in the school at the present time. At the same time that the student is contending with increasing pressures in the school, he or she must assume more responsibility in spheres of their life that are both within and outside the school. Probably at no time in our history have children been asked to be more responsible for themselves with the family abdicating many of its former functions to other social institutions, especially the school. Parents in certain aspects have become more permissive, and the family structure has weakened so that, in many instances, children's behavior and their outside activities often go totally unsupervised. Obviously, this situation promotes peer groups into very significant positions regarding young people's behavior. With the significant role played by peer groups, the significance of the school becomes even greater.

What emerges is the fact that the school is being asked, if not told, to do a great many activities that it is not set up to do. With the waning of the family influence, the school is thrust into a situation that it is not prepared to handle. Yet, it appears by abdication that the school must be a parent and now must decide if it will be a good parent.

In continuing to look for organizational factors that play a strong role in early school leaving and dropping out, we now turn to some findings of the classical High School and Beyond Study. Peng and Takai (1983) reported the following data for school-related reasons as to why students left school during the years 1980 to 1982.

School-Related Reasons

		Male	Female
		%	%
1	Expelled or suspended	13.0	5.3
2	Had poor grades	35.9	29.7
3	School was not for me	34.8	31.1
4	School grounds too dangerous	2.7	1.7
5	Didn't get into desired program	7.5	4.5
6	Couldn't get along with teachers	20.6	9.5

It appears that the most powerful "true" school response for both males and females is that "school was not for me." This rather general response shows up repeatedly throughout the research literature. Poor grades, on the other hand, which is equally as powerful as school-related reasons in explaining dropout behavior in this study, is in our opinion a much more diffuse concept in terms of what it explains and what explains it. Poor grades could just as easily be classified under the headings of health, family, or peer reasons for leaving school. Poor grades is not a pure concept when attempting to use it as an explanatory variable. There are many antecedent and intervening factors at work here. This further illustrates the myriad problems at work in trying to gain a handle on just who or what dropouts, pushouts, early school leavers, and at-risk children empirically are.

Peng (1985), in a later study using the same High School and Beyond data, noted that many educators think a high dropout rate is caused by a failure of the educational system to meet the aspirations and special needs of students.

To pursue this point a bit further, some organizational characteristics of alternative schools are presented. These characteristics could and should be part of the organizational climate of a regular public school. A further discussion of alternative schools is presented in Chapter 8. Butchcart (1986) lists the following three characteristics of alternative schools: (1) They attempt to foster academic and social comforts; (2) Friendly relationships between students and faculty are stressed; (3) Experiential learning is stressed. Raywid (1984) stressed the following elements as being important in alternative schools: (1) A substantial effort is likely to be addressed to create a strong sense of affiliation within the unit; (2) Structures and processes generated by school climate are held important and receive considerable attention within the unit; (3) Alternative schools generally address a broader range of student development than just the cognitive or academic. Typically, the sort of person a learner is becoming is a matter of first concern.

Further it may be noted by Butchcart (1986) that alternative schools generally are small in size, reducing the bureaucratization and impersonality found in many public schools. This small size tends to facilitate closer personal relationships between a student and his or her peers, the faculty, and the activities of the institution. At the same time, the research literature tends to reflect that one key to success with dropouts reentering through alternative education is in the quality of the relationships that can be created in an alternative school.

Dr. Jerry Morton, Director of the Alternative Center for Learning in Knoxville, Tennessee, continually stresses the importance of the good mental health of teachers. He feels that the educational system creates unhealthy adults (teachers) who foster their unhealthiness on students. This he sees as being a direct result of the school system. The ultimate result here can only be burnout of the teachers and poor learning or early school leaving, psychologically and then physically by the students.

ORGANIZATIONAL THEORIES

This chapter began with the research literature on why students leave school, focusing on individual reasons. We will conclude the chapter by looking at organizational theories that give some basis to what we have said in this section about school-related reasons for children leaving school.

Classical Theories

When one thinks of the classical theories of organizational development, one must first consider the works of Max Weber. Weber's ideal structure, developed in the late nineteenth and early twentieth centuries, included high degrees of specialization and impersonality, authority based on comprehensive rules rather than on social relationships, clear and centralized hierarchies of authority and responsibility, prescribed systems of rules and procedures, hiring and promotion based solely on technical ability, and extensive use of written documentation.

Weber saw this pure system as a historical trend that would meet the needs posed by the increasing size of organizations and that would at the same time replace unfairness and uncertainty with rationality and clarity. Sofer (1972) summarizes the advantages of bureaucracy as Weber saw them including the following: rationality, precision in operation, speed, reduction of friction between people, steadiness, subordination of juniors to seniors in a strict and known way, reliability, employees being trained to become experts in their particular fields, and gaining a habitual and virtuoso-like mastery of their subjects.

Weber's ideal bureaucracy in which the men/women at the top can make a decision and be confident that the organization will move with speed and precision to carry it out is still the goal of many practical administrators. Many of them accept his view that an organization must be built on: (1) specialization; (2) a hierarchy of officials, each of whom possesses a planned amount of authority; (3) impersonal rules; and (4) managers trained for their jobs (Dale, 1969). A human service agency, such as the school, designed on the basis of classical principles, would be organized so that all employees including professionals, paraprofessionals, and clerical workers perform regular specialized tasks.

Human Relations Approaches

The human relations approach to organizations assumes that the bureaucratic view of human beings is too narrow to be useful in real-life organizations. As Argyris (1957) points out, workers are really motivated by many factors other than economics, including desires for growth and independence. To Argyris, the organizational forms mandated by the classical theorists make for immature, dependent, and passive employees with little control over their work and thwart more mature employees capable of autonomy and independence. The purpose of the human relations approach is to develop organizational forms that build on worker's strengths and motivation (Lewis & Lewis, 1983).

A strength of the human relations approach for human service agencies such as schools is its consistency with the approach of helping professionals. Human service workers, especially teachers, tend to favor increasing self-responsibility and options for their clients. There is consistency in their work environments if they too are treated as responsible adults and if they have the chance to treat their coworkers and students in the same way (Lewis & Lewis, 1983).

Contingency Theories

The contingency theorists make clear that an effective organization can run the gamut from a traditional bureaucracy to a highly organized, constantly changing structure. Which structure is appropriate depends on the organization's needs. Lawrence and Lorsch (1967) stress that effective organizations have a good fit with their environment. An organization with a stable environment can use formal rules, a short-term horizon, traditional communication channels, and task-oriented management. An organization with an unstable environment needs more points of contact with the external world so that changes can be recognized promptly. Such an organization needs a longer time orientation and a more complex communication pattern. Formal rules and hierarchies would interfere with the needed information flow, so it would be inappropriate to rely on them (Lewis & Lewis, 1983).

The contingency theories, unlike the other approaches, recognize the impact of the external environment on each organization's structure and process. They are, in effect, systems theories. These ideas have been developed further in approaches that also see organizations primarily as open systems theories.

Open Systems Theory

The open systems theory sees the following nine points as being critical: (1) the importance of energy or input; (2) throughput; (3) output; (4) cycles of events; (5) negative entropy; (6) information input, negative feedback, and the coding process; (7) the steady state in dynamic homeostasis; (8) differentiation; and (9) equa-finality.

Theory Z

William Ouchi (1982) developed the Theory Z concept through a study of Japanese corporations. Assuming that there must be some organizational reason for Japanese workers' productivity and commitment, he studied a number of corporations. His findings were that Japanese organizations are characterized by lifetime employment, slow evaluation and promotion, non-specialization career path, collective decision-making styles, collective responsibility, and an integration between work and social lives. These characteristics can be contrasted with those of an American bureaucratic structure: short-term employment, rapid evaluation and promotion, specialization, explicit control mechanisms, individual decision making, individual responsibility, and segmented concern. The American worker, according to Ouchi, is more oriented toward his or her specialization than toward loyalty to the specific organization. In the United States, we conduct our careers between organizations but within a single specialty. In Japan, people conduct careers between specialties but within a single organization (Ouchi, 1982). The Theory Z emphasis on development of a central philosophy and on giving workers the opportunity to experience several parts of the organization might help build commitment and enhance mutuality in the agency's work.

These five approaches to organizational theory should tie up the variety of ways of looking at dropping out, ranging from the individual and the characteristics associated with it, to the school and the characteristics associated with it.

The following interview illustrates how teachers working within the system feel frustrated in trying to work with at-risk dropout-prone students. The interview shows that much of their frustration comes from the school system itself. The lack of interagency cooperation and teamwork is also illustrated. The second interview is with two quiet school leavers.

These students cause no problems and just quietly drift away. The school knows who these quiet school leavers are but appears incapable of gaining their interest or keeping them in school.

George Washington High School

In surveying the dropout problem, we have attempted to gather information from as many relevant sources as possible. They include students, administrators, and teachers. The information from teachers regarding at-risk youth is interesting, in that it reflects concerns that operate on several levels. On the system level, teachers report few if any options in trying to reach that child who is not learning. One assistant principal reported that she was spending 95 percent of her time on 5 percent of the children. These five percenters were also consuming all of her energy.

This assistant principal would like to see these children out of the system but not necessarily expelled. She speaks favorably of alternative schools and claims there ought to be more. She says it's worth it if I can work with the other 95 percent of the students.

A teacher says that expulsion and truancy hearings may not be ideal, but they serve the purpose of getting the parents' attention. On the other hand, regarding the parents' view on the students dropping out, this same teacher says, "The parents, quite frankly, in our school, generally support that (the student's dropping out). A lot of them think in the same way—I dropped out and I got a job." This teacher goes on to say this would be all well and good if these students had the requisite skills, vocational and social, but they don't.

The lack of options open to teachers, administrators, and students shows up as frustration for the teacher. This frustration must eventually lead to burnout. As one senior teacher told me, "You know, I was raised to be responsible. If I am supposed to teach you, I prepare and teach whether you learn or not. I do the part I am supposed to." Her sense of responsibility turns to frustration and eventually to burnout. Is her frustration with the system, the student, or is it all tied together? Another teacher shows her frustration when she says, "I don't know if we need to change. For those kids who want to know, there's nothing that will ever replace one who knows ... the teacher." The lecture method and being involved works with this student. "But there are some kids for whom that does not work (the lecture method) and there are more and more of them every year. Yet we try to put these little round pegs in square holes. It used to work much better than it is working now. We've got to have some relief."

John Adams High School

This interview is with two young girls who might be described as quiet school leavers. Our first young girl, Sandy, does nothing to get in trouble and is not a problem for teachers while she is in school. She is the second of two children, has an older brother, and her parents and brother both graduated from high school. Both of her parents work and have completed training beyond high school. Her brother was an athlete and graduated from high school with honors. He flunked out of college in his first year. It is a safe assumption that after her brother's failure the parents lost a great deal of interest in whether our subject, Sandy, did well in school or not.

Sandy is presently a junior in high school and is dating someone ten years older than she. She has held a job where she works 40 hours a week and has stayed out of school to work a day shift for up to one week. Sandy failed both the first and the second grade. One of the reasons she failed, she says, is because she read too fast. Her present feeling about school is clearly expressed when she says, "I wish I could get school over with and leave."

Sandy's report of her home life is somewhat inconsistent, in that at one point she says, "I have a problem with my daddy and my mother. They want me to leave." At another point, however, she says that the family is close, that they respect each other, and that they each do their own thing. Sandy says, "I know that they love me." It is our impression that this home has a swinging door, with Sandy coming and going as she pleases. Her parents appear to care very little whether she is in the home or not. At 16 she moved out and worked 40 hours a week to support herself. This did not last long, however, and she returned home to live.

While living at home, few demands are placed on her according to her report, and she dates a man ten years her senior. Her peer group does not exist in school but rather revolves around the older friends that she makes through her boyfriend. As might be expected, Sandy belongs to or participates in only one school activity and that is softball.

This young lady, along with the one who follows, was selected by asking the school to find some quiet school leavers. The two were easily found. Sandy is the type of student one should not lose. She is bright, articulate, and a hard worker.

Our next student, Sylvia, is a truant as well as a quiet school leaver. She is acutely aware of her feelings about school when she says, "Well, I don't like school and I ain't doing too well." She reports that she hasn't thought about what she will do if she doesn't finish school, but says that she has no skills to aid her in the world of work. Sylvia reports from early on that she didn't like school. As she says, "See, when I was little, I never did like school."

Sylvia's family life bears some resemblance to that of our other student, in that neither her mother nor stepfather ask about or check schoolwork. Her mother did not graduate from high school. She reports no contact with her father. She says she does not get along too well at home, and she and her mother fuss over school.

In regards to school rules, Sylvia does not believe that they are fair; she has had problems being on time and as she says throughout, "I just don't like school." Sylvia says, "I don't want to go to school right now. I get up in the morning and I fuss with my mom. I don't want to go and I look for an excuse. Then Mr. Smith told my mom if I don't start coming, I'm going to Juvenile." Sylvia continues, "I mean, you know, you can't be late, and if you're late, you get detention. Already got two of these." Sylvia dislikes school so much she will do almost anything to keep from going, including starting arguments with her mother in the morning that most certainly will make her late, which leads to detention and eventually to juvenile court. Sylvia had a difficult time understanding how she could be sent to juvenile court for not going to school.

The relationship between the juvenile court and the school system regarding truancy hearings is one of strain. The school wants the court to be the villain in these hearings, and the court resists. The court feels that it has enough to deal with when it comes to delinquents and is ill at ease in playing the heavy with regards to status offenders such as truants.

Both Sandy and Sylvia are quiet school leavers, and though they are different in some ways, they also share significant similarities, the strongest being that they drift away from school, without causing anybody other than themselves any real problems.

Chapter 8

DELINQUENCY AND DROPOUTS

I n dealing with the at-risk or dropout child, issues of delinquency and emotional disturbance become important focal points of the study.

Some research studies report delinquency and dropout as two options to dealing with stress or frustration. Other studies see delinquency and dropout as part of a feedback looping process. The consensus appears to be that delinquency leads to dropout which leads to delinquency. According to Elliott and Voss (1974), the adjudicated delinquent is usually a dropout.

Dropout, Delinquency, and Emotional Disturbance

In looking at the relationship between dropout, delinquency, and emotional disturbance, definitions of each are helpful. Some relevant theories on how these behaviors developed are presented later in this chapter. Succinct definitions using working concepts are used in defining dropout, delinquency, and child mental illness.

Dropout is defined as leaving school before graduating for any reason other than death. The rate is sometimes determined by subtracting the number of graduates from the number of students who were enrolled in the ninth grade four years earlier.

Delinquency is classified into two parts: (1) delinquent offenses and (2) status offenses. Delinquent offenses are those offenses that if committed by an adult would be a crime. They include murder, rape, arson, and assault. The charge in many of these cases includes a transfer hearing where the youth is tried as an adult in criminal court. Status offenses are those offenses that only a youth can commit. These include truancy, being beyond the control of the parent, unruliness, and curfew violations.

The status offense of truancy is of concern to us at this point and a petition can be filed by the school or parent charging the child with being truant and requiring a hearing at juvenile court. Putting a child on probation for truancy and then having the child violate the probation now allows the court to place the status of delinquent on the child for breaking rules of probation, not for being truant. While all this is going on, the child has probably been suspended or expelled from school. This may have the effect of pushing the child further into delinquency. Although, as stated later in this chapter, as dropout goes up, delinquency tends to go down. This is obviously a conundrum which will need further research than is possible in this text.

Childhood mental illness has the following definition under the Tennessee Code Annotated:

33-6-104. "Substantial likelihood of serious harm" defined—Standards for commitment to involuntary care and treatment.

(a) IF AND ONLY IF

  (1)(A) a person has threatened or attempted suicide or to inflict serious bodily harm on himself, OR

    (B) the person has threatened or attempted homicide or other violent behavior, OR

    (C) the person has placed others in reasonable fear of violent behavior and serious physical harm to them, OR

    (D) the person is unable to avoid severe impairment or injury from specific risks, AND

  (2) there is substantial likelihood that such harm will occur unless the person is placed under involuntary treatment;

THEN

  (3) the person poses a "substantial likelihood of serious harm" for purposes of 33-6-103 and this section.

  (b) IF AND ONLY IF

  (1) a person is mentally ill, AND

  (2) the person poses a substantial likelihood of serious harm because of the mental illness, AND

  (3) the person needs care, training, or treatment because of the mental illness, AND

  (4) all available less drastic alternatives to placement in a hospital or treatment resource are unsuitable to meet the needs of the person,

THEN

  (5) the person may be judicially committed to involuntary care and treatment in a hospital or treatment resource in proceedings conducted in conformity with part 6, Chapter 3 of this title.

    (c) No defendant may be judicially committed under this statute unless two (2) licensed physicians file in the commitment proceeding certificates of need for care and treatment certifying that the defendant satisfied the requirements of subdivisions (1)–(4) of subsection (b) and showing the factual foundation for the conclusions on each item.

(d) The parent, guardian, spouse, or a responsible adult relative of the person alleged to be in need of care and treatment, a licensed physician, a licensed clinical psychologist who meets the requirements of 33-6-103(f), a health or public welfare officer, an officer authorized to make arrests in Tennessee, or the head of any institution which the person is in may file a complaint to require involuntary care and treatment of a mentally ill person under this section.

(e) If the department has designated a licensed state facility as having available suitable accommodations, the court shall commit the defendant to the state facility, and the defendant shall be placed in the custody of the commissioner.

(f) If a licensed public hospital or treatment resource other than a state facility has available suitable accommodations, the court may commit the defendant to the public facility.

(g) If a licensed private or local public hospital or treatment resource has contracted with the department to serve such defendants in the region and has available suitable accommodations, the court shall commit the defendant to the facility, and the facility shall admit and detain the defendant in conformity with its obligations under its contract with the department.

(h) IF

(1)(A) a parent, guardian, spouse, or an adult relative of the defendant, or any other person has made arrangements to pay the cost of care and treatment in a licensed private hospital or treatment resources, OR

(B) such a facility chooses to accept the defendant despite the fact that no third person has made arrangements to pay the cost, AND

(2) placement in the facility is more appropriate to the needs of the defendant than placement in a state facility,

THEN

(3) the court may commit the defendant to the facility.

(i) The superintendent of a facility to which a person is committed under this section shall not admit the person until the facility has an available suitable accommodation. If a person is committed to a state facility under this section, the person does not come into the custody of the commissioner until the facility has an available suitable accommodation.

In a recent report by the Tennessee Department of Mental Health and Mental Retardation, it was reported that Tennessee overutilized hospital beds for children at a rate of 141.8 percent. Tennessee had an admission rate of 65.7 per 100,000 of state population. Only 7 of the states reporting have more hospital admissions per 100,000 of general population than Tennessee.

It may well be that the authors are living in an atypical state, but incarceration rather than outpatient or intermediate care possibly occurring in the schools is being overutilized.

From a sociological viewpoint, strain and control theory bear directly on dropouts and delinquency. In its simplest form, strain theory maintains that the school is a central force in the creation of problems for the child and plays a key role in his or her dropping out or becoming involved in delinquency. By removing him or herself from the source of the strain, the school, and returning to a more comfortable environment of the home and/or neighborhood, the individual may actually experience an increase in self-esteem (Agnew, 1985).

Control theory maintains that by keeping the young person in school, his or her behavior is controllable and deviant behavior, especially delinquency, is held down. Control theory advocates the importance of the institution, in our case the school, and the behavioral choices of the individual.

Elliott and Voss (1974) contrast the dropout and delinquents in the following manner. Dropouts were seen to: (1) fail to achieve desired goals; (2) be intro punitive; (3) experience social isolation; and (4) be exposed to pro-dropout influences. Delinquents, on the other hand, were characterized by: (1) real or anticipated failure; (2) extra punitiveness; (3) normlessness; and (4) extensive exposure to delinquent persons or groups. These behaviors are responses to failure, alienation, and selective exposure to the forms of behavior, either dropping out or delinquency (Elliott & Voss, 1974).

In testing the four sets of hypotheses for dropout and delinquency, Elliott and Voss (1974) found support only for anomie (normlessness). They report the form of alienation most conducive to delinquency is normlessness, and the critical context is the school. This adds further explanatory power to strain theory, as the school provides this type of alienation that is expressed in the form of normlessness. Strain theory sees delinquency as a response to the adolescents' perceived failure to satisfy basic social and psychological needs or to achieve a meaningful position within a social context, in our case, the school. Strain theory posits that dropout and delinquency are alternate responses to the strains generated by failure to achieve valued goals, and dropout is precipitated by aspiration-opportunity disjunction.

Two important sociological theories emerge at this point to go along with strain and control theory. They are anomie theory and differential association.

Anomie theory as developed by Robert Merton (1957) emphasizes social structure in explaining human behavior and sees behavioral choices as cultural or social options based on means and goals within society. The paradigm developed by Merton and based on cultural goals and institutional means sees social deviance as being largely a disjunction between means and goals. In other words, social deviance, in our case dropout, is based on the denial of goals and the denial or inaccessibility to socially approved means to reach these goals. The paradigm, as conceived by Merton (1968), is as follows:

	Means	*Goals*
Conformity	accept	accept
Innovation	reject	accept
Ritualism	accept	reject
Retreatism	reject	reject
Rebellion	accept & reject	accept & reject

The dropout would most likely be classified in the retreatist category. The retreatist denies the goals of society while at the same time denying the means to these goals. The innovator accepts the goals but denies or is denied access to the means that are approved to achieve these goals. Delinquency would easily fit within the innovator option. Delinquents often want what society says is desirable and good; they just don't believe in working for these cultural goals or they don't have the requisite skills to appropriately acquire what they want. The innovator option is an example of socially created deviance where the person has been socialized to the goals of society but does not have the appropriate skills to properly attain those goals that have been defined by society as necessary. Ritualism involves the rejection of goals but the acceptance of institutional means in order to reach those goals. An example of ritualism would be the farmer who holds on to the traditional ways of doing things, not being too concerned with output or productivity. The rebellion alternative involves the rejection of both means and goals but the establishment of new goals and new means. This alternative might include those who would favor the redistribution of wealth based on some new economic formula. Conformity would be where both goals and the means toward those goals are accepted. The virtue of hard work and desiring what society says is important is an example of the conformity option. These categories refer to role behaviors and specific types of situations, not personality types.

The aim of this paradigm is to discover how some social structures exert a definite pressure upon certain persons in the society to engage in non-conforming rather than conforming conduct. As mentioned, normlessness was a strong finding relating to dropout. It is defined as when one interactant (a student) cannot fathom any meaning from the other's behavior (teacher) and thus is left in a state of diffuse anxiety and fear. Such is likely to occur when the interactants (student and teacher) employ entirely different mentally impenetrable universes of discourse and gesture (Scott & Lymon, 1970). It is this state of anomie that appears to be of great importance in trying to understand the dynamics of dropout and delinquency.

Differential association, the other theoretical approach found to have explanatory power regarding dropouts and delinquency, lists the following steps as explaining how deviant behavior is learned. The theory has a long predictive history regarding delinquency and crime; how well it explains dropout behavior is the quest of this chapter.

Differential association states that:

1. Criminal behavior is learned.
2. Criminal behavior is learned in interaction with others in a process of communication.
3. The principle part of the learning of criminal behavior occurs within intimate personal groups.
4. When criminal behavior is learned, the learning includes:
   a. techniques of committing the crime, which are sometimes very complicated, sometimes very simple;
   b. the specific direction of motives, drives, rationalizations, and attitudes.
5. The specific direction of motives and drives is learned from definitions of the legal codes as favorable or unfavorable.
6. The person becomes delinquent because of an excess of definitions

favorable to violation of law, over definitions unfavorable to violation of law.

7. Differential association may vary in frequency, duration, priority,
and intensity.

8. The process of learning criminal behavior by association with criminal and anti-criminal patterns involves all of the mechanisms that
are involved in any other learning. (Sutherland & Cressey, 1970)

Theoretically, these four approaches, strain theory, control theory,
anomie theory, and differential association, offer explanatory power for
the understanding of dropout and delinquents. Hypotheses following
from these approaches are:

1. Failure in school institutes a search for more satisfying group
membership which typically results in the acquisition of delinquent friends (differential association).

2. Dropping out is a consequence of internal attribution of blame,
social isolation, and experiences that influence the dropout (differential association).

3. If failure in school leads to delinquency, then dropping out of
school should result in decreasing involvement in delinquency
(strain theory). The research of Elliott and Voss (1974) did not find
a great deal of support for the theoretical models presented here.
Nonetheless, even though this is an outstanding study, our belief is
that these models merit further research. These approaches on face
would appear to have value in regards to gaining greater understanding of dropouts. They have been shown to have explanatory
relevance in regards to delinquency in the past.

Another theoretical approach that has been shown to have strong
explanatory power in the areas of delinquency and emotional disturbance is labeling theory (Schur, 1981; Gove, 1974).

Labeling theory posits that human behavior is a response to one of
three audiences: (1) society at large; (2) those persons, including significant others, with whom a person has daily interaction; and (3) official
and organizational agents of social control (Schur, 1971).

The following constructs may be considered to be at the heart of
labeling theory and should guide us along in trying to gain greater
understanding of at-risk youth, dropouts, delinquents, and emotionally
disturbed youth:

1. The basic premise is that deviance is a socially created category.

2. The consequent primary focus should be on societal reaction,

rather than on the characteristics of deviance or other perpetuating factors influencing the deviating individual.

3. An attempt should be made to understand deviance from the viewpoint of the deviant rather than that of society at large.
4. The importance of the definition of the situation is to be remembered by human service workers. The fact that these definitions are sometimes negotiated is to be recognized.
5. Careful observation is the basic research technique to be utilized.

Labeling, like anomie theory, has been shown to be an effective way in which to conceptualize delinquency or emotional disturbance. Many of its premises can be applied to dropout and eventually tested.

The fact that dropout, pushout, truancy, or early school leaver is a socially constructed category seems incontrovertible. As shown in Chapter 6, how dropouts are categorized by social control agents plays a large role in definition and makes comparisons difficult. In Chapter 6, we also make the point that dropping out may be more a result of the school than the student and that focusing on the school, along with the student, should provide greater understanding than focusing solely on the student as is so often the case. Labeling theory, by placing emphasis on the agencies of social control, allows us to avoid the "blaming the victim" ideology described by William Ryan (1971).

Case studies which are presented in Chapters 6 and 8 utilize techniques designed to determine how the actor defines his or her situation. The purpose here is to learn from the student *how* they see they became at risk in their school lives. How people create their own reality or define their own situations is what social science tries to determine regardless of the method that is used. This book relies on quantitative as well as qualitative methods. Nonetheless, careful observation, interviewing, and shagging [hanging around (Goetz & LeCompte, 1984)] are all being used to get at how the at-risk student defines his or her situation. William I. Thomas (1967) said that if you define a situation as real, it is real in its consequences.

Delinquency and mental health are important to the understanding of dropout, because so often these behaviors become intertwined with each other, and time order becomes difficult to determine. From a theoretical perspective, this is a teasing set of questions. From a human service perspective, the issue becomes a concrete one of how best to design and deliver service.

It is our contention that because correctional and mental health facilities in Tennessee and throughout the nation are filled, children with
behavioral problems that were formally served by those departments,
meaning mental health and corrections, now must be served by the
school system. Our belief is that by intervening and treating at-risk
dropouts, preventing pushouts, and becoming aware much earlier of
early school leavers, *prevention* will occur regarding potential delinquents and emotionally disturbed children. As mentioned earlier, time
order is difficult to determine with complex variables like these, but it is
our assumption that early intervention in schools translates to prevention in corrections and mental health.

Given all that has been said in this chapter, it is our contention that
theoretically and from a human services perspective, dropout and delinquency and emotional disturbance all hang together. Young clients who
are being served by one of these agencies are just as likely to be seen by
one or more of the others. That is, a troubled youth in corrections may
have emotional problems that are also related to problems in school.
Multi-agency task forces designed to treat troubled youth come and go,
but the fact that school, juvenile court, mental health and welfare must
continually interact in order to meet the needs of children and youth is
indisputable.

SUMMARY DISCUSSION

To conclude, let us recapitulate the thrust of this chapter. The central
point is that even though time order and causality are most difficult to
determine when dealing with dropout, delinquency, and child mental
health, it seems worthwhile to assume that there are strong correlations
among the three. It also appears that the simplest and most worthwhile
place to make early interventions is the school. Our assumption as stated
earlier in this chapter is that early and appropriate intervention in the
school allows for prevention of delinquency and emotional disturbance.
This proposal is corroborated by Lloyd (1978) who used longitudinal
data in predicting dropouts from looking at their third grade records.
The school is a place where future problems can be warded off in regards
to delinquency and child emotional disturbance.

One possible reason for not doing early intervention or pursuing
primary prevention is that of the phenomenon of the self-fulfilling
prophecy (Merton, 1968). The self-fulfilling prophecy in our case would

involve bringing about occurrences that we are in fact trying to prevent. That is, the intervention aimed at the early at-risk child might actually cause the child to leave school when in reality that child was not at risk for leaving. The concept of iatrogenics is at work here when the intervention actually made things worse. That is, the client is worse off because of what was done to or for him or her. To use an old phrase, "The operation was a success, but the patient died."

Nonetheless, it is our contention that well-thought-out early intervention is the way to go. These interventions, along with other strategies, are discussed throughout the text. The research of Elliott and Voss (1974) reflects that theory generated to explain delinquency is much further along than theory designed to explain and predict dropout. As they say at the conclusion of their study, "The guiding proposition for this study was that delinquent behavior and dropout are alternative responses to failure and alienation and are influenced by selective exposure to such behavior." They report that the strongest predictors of dropout are academic failure, school normlessness and social isolation, exposure to dropout in the home, and commitment to peers. The major instigating forces of dropout are found to be academic failure and alienation from school. They found that there was an inverse relationship between dropout and delinquency. That is, as dropouts increased, delinquency decreased. This led to the conclusion that the school is a generating milieu for delinquency.

It is not a coincidence that the rate of delinquency is inversely related to the rate of dropout. As the holding power of our schools has increased, so has the rate of delinquency. Compulsory school attendance facilitates delinquency by forcing youths to remain in what is sometimes a frustrating situation in which they are stigmatized as failures. It is not surprising that these youth trapped in our schools rebel or attempt to escape. In the final analysis, escape either through dropout or graduation appears to be the only satisfactory resolution of this problem. For the dropout and the graduate, rates of delinquency decline upon leaving the compulsory school setting. Delinquency, on the other hand, is not an adequate solution but serves only to set in motion reciprocal processes of rejection and alienation and thereby increases the probabilities of failure.

It does not necessarily follow from these observations that all students who are alienated and frustrated by their experiences in school or who perceive the school as meaningless should be encouraged to drop out of high school. However, in some cases, this may be an appropriate course of action and should not be restricted by law. A more important strategy would be to change the structure of the school to explore new types of learning environments in which competition is minimized and in which failure ceases to be a functional prerequisite of the educational system (Elliott & Voss, 1974).

Chapter 9

ALTERNATIVE CENTER FOR LEARNING*

Alternative School Data

The following profile of at-risk students is derived from question-naire data gathered from 143 students referred to the Alternative Center for Learning (ACL) during the years 1987 through 1989. The students and their parents were asked to sign a waiver before filling out the questionnaire. Filling out the questionnaire was voluntary and there were no penalties for not participating. The mean age of students is 15.8 years. Eighty-one percent are white; nineteen percent are black. Seventy percent of the students are male and thirty percent are female. The majority of the students are in the tenth grade when they are referred to the school. Most come from blue-collar homes where their mothers did not graduate from high school. The mothers averaged 11.84 years of school while the fathers averaged 12.14 years of schooling.

Thirty-three point six percent of the sample reported living with both parents. The other 66.4 percent reported living with one parent, step-parents, other relatives, or friends. It seems that the students come from family situations that add to them being at risk in school as well as in other social situations. Forty-four percent of the students report that their parents are married, the remaining report being separated, widowed, or divorced. Forty-five percent report living with their mother.

The students state that family is important to them and that their parent(s) want them to finish school, but they do not report living in environments that approach the ideal that they say they want. Eighty-five percent report that "family is very important to me." This family constellation variable is a very important one. We caution, however, that the family situation should not be seen as an insurmountable object by the school. It simply means that the school will have to take on more than it presently is and that support from the community will have to be enlarged. At one point, this may have seemed naive. Now, with the

---

*Note: A major contribution to this chapter was made by Dr. Jerome H. Morton, Director of the Alternative Center for Learning, Knoxville, Tennessee.

increased awareness of the dropout problem, it is imperative rather than naive.

In describing our at-risk population, comparisons to what have been found elsewhere are important. Thus, some further details are presented on our subjects. Seventy-six point three percent report very little participation in athletics. Eighty-seven percent say the same about band or chorus. It is our contention that non-participation in school activities is highly correlated with early school leaving. Other studies have drawn support for this correlation, but some have not. It is our belief that involving students in school activities is a hedge against dropping out. Involving students in school activities is also something that can be done by the school. Involvement is a key social need of these young people.

Compliant behavior tends to be rewarded by schools. In fact, rule following appears to be either more important or a necessary prerequisite to graduation, depending on how responses are interpreted. Kauffman (1989) found the following to be skills critical for success in regular classrooms. In descending order of importance, they are:

1. Follows established classroom rules.
2. Listens to teacher instructions.
3. Can follow teacher-written instructions and directions.
4. Complies with teacher commands.
5. Does in-class assignments as directed.
6. Avoids breaking classroom rules even when encouraged by a peer.
7. Produces work of acceptable quality given his or her skill level.

These above items were rated critical for success by over 51 percent of secondary school teachers in a study by Kerr and Zigmond (1986). It is noteworthy that the six items rated above quality of work are directly or indirectly related to school rule and rule-following behavior. Nine point one percent of the students referred to ACL report that they follow rules at school most of the time. Ninety point nine percent report some difficulty in following school rules. For the school, following rules is of utmost importance; the same cannot be said for this type of student. The question we must be concerned with is just how many of our students challenge rules that they perceive as unfair and commit an act of primary deviance (questioning of rules) and then become labeled as behavior disordered, truant, or dropout, an act of secondary deviance.

Along with not participating in school activities, another predictor of school failure is being in the right age grade. Fifty-five point nine percent of our sample say they are not in the right grade for their age, and 60.1 percent acknowledge that they have failed at least one grade. This variable is one that can and should be targeted for early intervention. When variables are easily seen, it would make sense to intervene on a concrete level at an early point, no later than third grade if the child has failed a grade by this time. As soon as failure occurs, intervention should be made, if not sooner.

Truancy is a target behavior to look for as a precursor to early school failure. Absenteeism, according to our sample, occurs on the average of 1.15 days per week. This is especially interesting since only 18.2 percent of the students report being sick a lot. Truancy is certainly a warning signal for continued problems in school.

If a child is truant, one assumption might be that the child finds school uninteresting, unlikable, or not challenging. Students from our sample reported generally that they do not like school. Sixteen point one percent reported that they like school most of the time. Eighty-three point nine percent said they like school some of the time or never. Thirty point one percent reported that school was boring.

Pregnancy is cited throughout the literature as being a primary reason for females to leave school. Males, on the other hand, do not report leaving to support the new babies about to be born. Hence, most of these babies will come into the world to be raised by children, and single-parent children at that.

Over the two-year period that we have been gathering data from our sample, we have consistently found that pregnancy is *not* a good reason to leave school, according to our respondents. Eighteen point two percent of our sample reported that getting pregnant was a good way of getting out of going to school.

Why our data on pushouts do not support the numerous other studies' findings on pregnancy is open to various interpretations. It might be that Southern girls see themselves as self-reliant and capable of raising these children. The extended family of the South may also play a role in the girls' choice of raising the baby. Abortion is generally not considered an option by our female respondents. Our findings may also be an artifact of the attitude behavior dichotomy where an attitude is not carried over into behavior. The evidence seems to be that we have pregnant teenagers and they are not staying in school.

Drug use certainly is a correlate of problems in school. But correlation is definitely not causation. Yet the following percentages yield some interesting results. When asked a Murphy and Likert (1937) type question, only 7 percent of our population report using drugs most of the time. On a yes/no question, 45 percent reported using drugs. It may be that our population is a moderate user of drugs or has tried drugs at least once. Drugs for these students, including alcohol and cigarettes, may be a result rather than a cause of school problems. Our respondents report smoking is "not cool" (82%), yet the vast majority of them do it.

After-school jobs are often correlated with school problems. Many youth report working 30 hours or more per week. Our population does not fit the model of working or being needed at home. Forty-seven percent report that they do not work at all. This may be due to the age of the group (15.8 years), or more likely that they don't have the technical or social skills to obtain and/or hold a job. At the same time, 35 percent state that their parents need them at home. This same group says that they enjoy working for what they want (84%), and money and power are important to them (74%). As throughout this section, one can see crosscurrents running through these results.

Another variable that the literature cites as important to staying in school is family support. Our sample of at-risk students saw their parents as being very supportive of their graduating from high school. Ninety-three percent state that their family wants them to graduate from high school. This sample of at-risk students certainly shows signs of being salvageable, and the alternative school where they are currently enrolled appears to be the mechanism that will keep them from dropping out or being pushed out of school.

When asked questions regarding the comparison of their feelings toward public school and the alternative school, striking differences occurred. When asked "At which school have you learned more?", the students reported 69.2 percent at the alternative school and 28.7 percent said at the regular school. When asked "Where have you learned more about life?", 67.8 percent said the alternative school, 11.9 percent said regular school, and a strong 20.3 percent did not answer. When asked "At which school have you learned more about career opportunities?", 51.7 percent said the alternative school, 22.4 percent said regular school, and a substantial number, 25.9 percent, did not respond. When asked "Where have you learned more about yourself?", only 8.4 percent reported regular school, 66.4 percent reported the alternative school, and 25.2 percent did not respond. The large percentage of non-responders gives us cause to be concerned, but it is our assumption that the responses would have been randomly distributed across opportunity choices. A more thorough investigation of the data is certainly called for and will be done in the future.

In studying the students' perceptions of the alternative school, 79 percent reported that the school had been beneficial to them in the education process, and 78.3 percent said yes regarding the growing process.

Thirty-eight point five percent reported looking forward to returning to their regular school, and 52.4 percent did not look forward to returning to their regular school. However, 58 percent reported not having returned to their regular school since being at the alternative school either to attend classes or to work on future attendance. The average time enrolled for students in the sample of 143 is nine months. The main reason reported for being referred to the alternative school is conflict, either with authorities or school rules, 10.5 and 30.1 percent.

In combining observational data with this questionnaire data, a good sense of the alternative school emerges.

A Profile

Introduction

Alternative Center for Learning (ACL) was created in 1980 by Knoxville City and Knox County School Systems to serve students who had been suspended or expelled from the regular school programs. ACL was originally funded by the state as a regional center for several school systems. Now, all of ACL's students come from the county school system because of changes in funding sources. State funding patterns shifted; systems now receive direct funding for discipline problem students. Also, the Knoxville City School System closed.

The ACL is a private, non-profit organization. Its board of directors was originally composed of administrators from the two school systems, a faculty member from The University of Tennessee at Knoxville, and the past superintendent of Knox County Schools, Dr. Mildred Doyle. Dr. Doyle died in May of 1989. The other original members are still on the ACL Board, although one has retired from the school system. Two other board members have been added to more accurately reflect the community at large.

ACL has always been a tool of the local school systems. Because of

ACL's flexibility, it is to Knox County School System's advantage to have ACL remain a private non-profit organization. The school system provides directly or indirectly almost all of ACL's funds and all of the students. All but one of the staff's salaries are paid through Knox County's payroll. Almost all of the donated supplies come from the system, and all of the building space is provided by it. Should Knox County Schools decide to terminate, the ACL would cease to exist.

Students who have been suspended or expelled from their regular schools and have been referred to ACL by school officials or adults may attend ACL if they choose to do so and if ACL has space available. Special education students assigned to ACL by multidisciplinary teams are also accepted if space allows. At any given time ACL serves about 70 students and serves a total of about 140 students each year.

From the very beginning ACL has focused on two major aspects of its students' needs: their emotional well-being and their academic progress. When a day-to-day choice has to be made between advancing the emotional well-being of the students and advancing their academic progress, the emotional well-being of the student has taken precedence. Limited funding, space, and changing student populations have caused ACL to make adjustments in programming for its students. ACL has evolved from being perceived as a holding center for bad kids to a healing center for young people with problems. This perceptual set shift has brought about the referral to ACL of a different type of student. In the beginning no children referred to ACL were categorized as handicapped. Today, 50 percent of its students are identified as handicapped, with learning disabled and seriously emotionally disturbed being the dominant categories of handicapping conditions.

Present Strategies

At this time, ACL's basic classroom consists of 15 students, a teacher, a teacher assistant, and a guidance counselor. The class functions more like a one-room school than like a typical high school. The 15 students can be a mixture of seventh through twelfth graders. There is an attempt to group the students into two grade levels within a classroom, but the needs of specific students and the various times that students come to ACL and leave prevent a consistent implementation of this policy. A goal of ACL is to send as many of its students as possible back to their regular schools and have them be successful both behaviorally and academically.

Supporting the basic classroom structure are a program coordinator, a general secretary, a records management person, a floating teacher assistant, a half-time director, a quiet room coordinator, a curriculum specialist, an artist in residence, and a foster grandmother. The school system has assigned a special education coordinator and provides additional services from specialists such as reading consultants and speech therapists on an as-needed basis.

Individualized instruction is a key to ACL's academic success for its students. For every student an individualized educational plan is implemented. Grouping does take place, but a particular child is involved in a given learning situation because of a specific educational need. This does not mean that each student functions in isolation all day. It means that the teacher knows the educational reason for each student participating in a learning process which includes his/her level of learning, his/her style of learning, and his/her rate of learning new information. Some of the students' instructional tasks are presented just to them while others are presented in a group process. When instruction is presented in the group process, each student is expected to respond at his or her academically appropriate level rather than at a predetermined group norm. This approach requires a tremendous amount of preplanning and carefully organized instructional materials. ACL does not feel it has perfected this instructional process and is constantly trying to improve.

A behavior modification token economy is also used to reward students. The staff attempts to focus on the positive aspects of the student and tries to make 80 percent of its evaluative statements be positive. The rationale for using the token economy is not that ACL thinks the students function totally on a stimulus-response basis but that the system demonstrates to the students that they can be successful and manifest totally new behaviors in a short period of time. Their perceptions of themselves alter. They see that they can change, that they do have control of their own behavior and can be the person they would like to be.

Another benefit of the token system is that it enables the teachers to play the role of cheerleaders encouraging the students on to success as opposed to being negative authority figures constantly punishing the students for not doing things right. The token economy is based on a positive reinforcement system patterned after the RAID program, which is the subject of a paper written for teachers by Ralph Bailey, of the Pinellas County, Florida school system, and Jerome Morton, of ACL. The acronym RAID (which stands for the words Rules, Approval, Ignore, Disapproval) was coined by Charles Madson of the University of Florida.

Being in your seat on time, completing a lesson, getting an A on an assignment are just some of the ways of earning points. The points are exchanged for privileges such as playing a game with someone, listening to a radio, or obtaining an early release from school. The students get immediate reinforcement for appropriate behaviors and learn that they can cause good things to happen for themselves. They do not view themselves as victims of circumstances constantly confronted with their failures.

The counselors collectively describe themselves as using immediate environment-oriented intervention techniques with the students. If the student makes a decision, the consequences of that decision within his or her subculture are explored. The focus is to assist the student in selecting behaviors that will accomplish his or her goals. Individual and group counseling sessions are scheduled for all students. In addition, crisis counseling sessions take place as needed. Outside specialists in areas such as sexual abuse, AIDS, street law, and employment are frequently brought in to speak to the students.

A significant component of the guidance program is utilizing the human services provided within the community. ACL interfaces with at least 19 different agencies and programs on a weekly basis. It could not begin to be as effective as it is without this assistance. Rather than seeing itself as a separate agency, it tries to perceive itself as an extension of the schools and the other human service agencies in a continuum of services. Approximately 60 percent of ACL's students are utilizing the services of other agencies and programs. These range from day psychiatric care counselors to juvenile court officials to group home supervisors. Close communications between ACL's staff and the staffs of the other programs is important if the maximum benefit of these services is to be realized by the students. Counselors, teachers, and other staff are constantly meeting with their counterparts in the other programs.

Another important characteristic of ACL is its commitment to the emotional well-being of its staff. It is imperative that the adults working with the students be emotionally balanced. By definition, the students are not. The staff will not be emotionally healthy by accident. ACL is a high stress environment. The administration and staff are actively involved in maintaining their emotional well-being.

All of ACL's students have helping jobs within their classroom. It is explained to every entering student that ACL is a community that exists with the help of its students. ACL does not have enough funds to keep the school clean or do a lot of the other things it does without the help of its students. Every student will have a job assigned to him/her. The student does not have to do the job, but ACL will be the lesser for it. Someone else will have to do the task if the student doesn't. It may be another student, the teacher or the director. Students can choose what job they'd like to do. Some jobs enable the student to earn points for their completion, while others require the student to pay points to have the privilege to do them. While the jobs are truly meaningful to the function of ACL, they also assist the student to become a valued and contributing part of a community. As mentioned earlier, a high percentage of these students have never been involved in any school activities before. This process is a beginning step in teaching the student how to function in a group.

The quiet room is a modification of the old time-out room concept. Rather than being a punitive place, the quiet room is a place that the student can withdraw from the continuous flow of activities taking place within ACL. The student can request to go to the quiet room at any time or a teacher can request that a student go there. The one requirement is that the student bring some academic assignments to work on. The student does not have to work on them while in the quiet room, but they must be available. Soft music, usually classical, is played in the room. There are magazines, crossword puzzles, and other individual tasks the student may choose to occupy his or her time. If the student wants to simply sleep at the desk, that is all right as well. The quiet room coordinator is always present to assist students with their lessons or simply to be a listening post for a frustrated person. When a teacher sends a student, the teacher is required to have a predetermined amount of time for the student to be there.

ACL's artist in residency program has been highly successful. A nationally recognized artist works with students in small groups and individually during the school day. The goal is not to make skilled artists out of the students but to allow them to express themselves more freely through the medium of art. Some students are selected to come to the art room on a scheduled basis while others can elect to come at times of crisis to use the art area as a tool in finding appropriate ways of expressing their frustrations. Several of ACL's students have won regional and national recognition for their art work.

Granny Gray is an institution all to herself as one of ACL's foster grandmothers. She has a special ability that allows her to communicate with some students that no one else can reach. She is at ACL every morning. Selected students visit her on a regular basis. For times of crisis, the students can request to go talk to their foster grandmother and will be allowed to do so immediately. The foster grandmother program is a real asset to ACL. It has had two foster grandmothers assigned to it, but the illnesses of the elderly ladies has reduced the total number of days they can be present. During their illnesses their students send them letters, art projects, and other tokens of their respect.

Different staff members are constantly sponsoring some special project. It may be a spring fashion show for the school, a school newspaper or yearbook, a trip to the art museum, or a canoe trip. Whatever it is, it requires the students' input to pull it off and staff members willing to supervise it. It also enhances the academic or counseling goals set for the participating students. The staff continually changes leadership roles in the projects. One project director in one activity may volunteer to supervise folding up the chairs after another activity.

Volunteers from the community enable ACL to do all that it does. Undergraduate and graduate students from The University of Tennessee, faculty members from the university and Knoxville College, parents of present and former ACL students, former ACL students, concerned citizens, and educators from other schools as well as many others give of their time, money, and resources to assist ACL. Some who give money or equipment wish to remain anonymous. Some give of their skills and labor. A retired Oak Ridge scientist may teach a special science subject; a former captain of the UT soccer team may teach soccer during PE; the mother of a former ACL staff member may cook a favorite dish for the field day buffet. Several UT students are assigned to ACL by their professors for course work requirements in such areas as counseling and human services during any given semester. The volunteers are so numerous that occasionally ACL must ask them to wait until a later date in order to coordinate their valuable assistance effectively.

Research on the effectiveness of ACL's delivery system is difficult to collect for several reasons. Strategy changes are continuously implemented as a result of lessons learned; the student population changes; funding fluctuates. However, information has been collected. In 1985, Dr. Robert Delozier conducted a study to see how many students had stayed in school, graduated, obtained a GED, or dropped out of school five years after their leaving ACL. Eighty-five percent of all seniors enrolled at ACL had graduated or obtained a GED. The lower grades had decreasing success down to the lowest grade, seventh, which had a 49 percent rate of successfully completing or staying in school. Given Knox County School's estimated dropout rate of 35 percent and the very high probability that ACL's students would have dropped out if they had not attended its program (projected 70 percent), the survey results are encouraging. ACL is in the process of starting another five-year study. The preliminary results are more encouraging than those of the previous five-year study. Perhaps the most significant results of ACL's program are reflected in the anecdotal statements of the students' home school staff, parents of ACL students, and the students themselves. The students constantly return to ACL to tell their teachers and counselors of their successes and frustrations in life. It is clear that they value ACL despite the fact that ACL was not nor is it now all that it would like to be. The greatest reason for success may be that students are matched with adults whose emotional health is relatively good and that a caring relationship is created between them.

There were some specific lessons learned during the school's formative years. One was to use the one-room-school classroom concept, which kept the students with the same teacher for the majority of the day and enabled the teacher and the student to form a close relationship. Another was to individualize instruction as much as possible. The student's self-concept was tied to his/her ability to be successful in completing class assignments. With individualized instruction, the teacher could present the opportunity for success at an appropriately challenging level. A third lesson was that ACL students don't benefit from academic instruction when they are emotionally upset. The emotional situation must be resolved for the student at an acceptable level if academic progress is to take place. An additional lesson was that an adult needed to be with the students constantly because of their poor impulse control. Another lesson was that the community in which ACL is located needs to be kept informed of ACL's mission and of the positive nature of its work. A sixth lesson was that the community human service agencies serving ACL students and the ACL staff must communicate if all of the efforts are to be productive. A truly disturbing lesson was to realize that a lot of very bad things happen to young people outside of the school environment; these occurrences must be addressed in counseling sessions. Facing the reality that ACL cannot assist every student because the needs of some students exceed the resources of the Center was another important lesson. Those students need to be referred to more appropriate programs as soon as possible. Finally, ACL learned that parent conferences or conferences with the significant adult in the child's life must take place before the child is admitted and before any significant changes or recommendations occur. If someone will not come in with the child, it is fairly certain that significant child neglect is taking place and appropriate actions need to be initiated.

Interviews

The following four interviews illustrate from the students' viewpoints what dropping out is all about. These people speak eloquently as to how they came to be at risk. The interview with students we have called "persisters" gives us hope for a certain segment of our high school population.

The first interview is typical of students we have studied for two years at the Alternative Center for Learning that most appropriately are labelled pushouts. Pushouts are not typical of dropouts in general, but they are a definite sample population of at-risk youth who do not fit within the public school sphere of influence. These students share much in common with the students who have already dropped out and are enrolled in a general education degree program at the Private Industrial Council. The general education degree students enrolled at the Private Industrial Council comprise our second interview. This interview illustrates the importance of keeping pathways back to school open.

The at-risk youths in interview 3 share much in common with interviews 1 and 2 but not much with interview 4.

To illustrate how different dropouts and pushouts are from persisters, interview 4, with very successful high school students, is presented. There is no doubt that there is a significant difference between the pushouts, dropouts, and at-risk youths and persisters.

Interview 1

Pushouts

This case study involves three students enrolled in an alternative school who have not dropped out at this point. The two males have had a history of problems with the public school and the law. The female is a first offender who was expelled for having a bottle of liquor in her car on school grounds. She has already returned to public school at this writing. The two males will stay at the alternative school for the entire school year. Where they will be next year will be determined by an M–Team staffing in the spring. At this point, we assume one will return to the public school next year and one will stay at the alternative school, the Alternative Center for Learning in Knoxville, Tennessee.

As to why the alternative school meets the needs of these students more effectively than the public school, one of them says, "This school here is to give us a last chance that we didn't think we had anymore. The schools we were going to was another way to take our money." These students go on to make the point that the teachers at the Alternative Center for Learning are more open: "They listen to you. These teachers accept you. I mean, they don't judge you for what you look like, they judge you for the person that you are. They give you a chance."

Another student reports that the sense of community that exists at the Alternative Center for Learning is the key to his staying in school. He says, "Everybody's here because they did something wrong. Ain't nobody here for being on the honor roll." He goes on to say that everyone is treated the same and there is no favoritism.

Favoritism is something these students have experienced in public school, but it has not been directed at them. As they report regarding cliques in the public school, the teachers definitely show who they like. This concept of teacher favoritism appears in several schools that we have investigated. It was even acknowledged by a group of students who received this favored treatment. The interesting point here is that the teachers appeared to cue on certain students based on messages that they receive from other students.

The existence of cliques and groups, variously labeled trendy, hood, nerd, jock, and thrasher, shows the importance of peer groups. Peer groups have a long history of being touted as causes of human behavior. In fact, peer groups in reference group theory have a lengthy bibliography covering many years. But the following quote illustrates a form of internal locus of control where the negative impact of peer groups may be ignored. "You can't learn nothing from your buddies, man. Nowadays your buddy don't convince you by 'Man, do this spelling and math. Come on, brother, let's go talk, act crazy.' That's what they want you to do, not to do your work."

Oftentimes throughout the literature dropouts are labeled as having an external locus of control, blaming others for their problems and, for females, that pregnancy was a good way to get out of going to school. Our sample of pushouts who we feel are a quite different subgroup tends to reflect an internal locus of control. They are per se a more internal aggressive group. Later, with the persister sample, we find a tendency to external locus of control. The female respondent, following along with this internal locus of control perspective, says in regards to money, "I don't want people handing things out to me. I don't like parents coming out and saying, 'Oh, here's this and this. I mean, that's so cruel." From a male perspective, pregnancy and parental responsibility are also viewed from an internal perspective. In regards to his possible child, one young man says, "Well, for one thing man, I ain't gonna walk off and leave it, I know that, cause man, I met my father when I was ten years old, man, it hurt me. I see from that how a boy would feel and a little girl would probably feel to meet their father at ten years old, man that's bullshit right there. I felt bad. I would just take him and whup up on him some."

Interview 2

GED Candidates

A view of how two eighteen-year-old men have come to see the world is illustrated in the following quotes. It would appear from the world view presented here that school is certainly not foremost in their values or their thinking. Speaking of his father, he says "He ain't trying to find a job or nothing. You know, we're seeing it hard. He thinks we can live off my aunt and shit, you know, we can't do that. You know, she got enough on her now. Trying to pay bills and shit and you know hell, that's the reason I came back here to get my GED and get a job so I can help them out." This young man illustrates the importance of keeping pathways open for those who have already dropped out of school as he has. He appears to want to have prosocial attitudes and to make contributions to his family. This is interesting, in that he had troubles in school and two brushes with the law. His friend gives him, from his viewpoint, sage advice when the conversation is continued and he says, "You need to help yourself out, man, don't worry about your parents. You give all your money to your parents . . . I used to do that, too. I used to have a job at another restaurant . . . I was the main cook. I was making six dollars an hour. I used to give all my money to my mom and she . . . you know it won't work out. You get tired of dealing with your momma. Cause you can't live with your momma or your parents all your life. I found that out when I was fifteen. That's when I moved out of my mom's house."

It has been our experience that many of these at-risk youth live in a home with a revolving door. Their parents have no idea if they are in the home or not. They are there one night and gone the next. Our sample reflects a great many young people who are living within these types of conditions. How could we expect anything less than dropping out of school in conditions like this?

Our second young man continues on with his philosophy of life and what we have called locus of control when he speaks about jail. "They don't have to worry about jail, the people I hang around with. Jail ain't shit to them. That's just a place to stay and feed them. They ain't worried about it. But you know if you don't . . . you know, help yourself out, ain't nobody gonna help you out. You want to be on welfare all your life . . . I feel sorry for you. Cause you ain't my friend saying you ain't gonna help yourself out. I don't like to be around nobody who ain't gonna help theirself out."

His friend replies back, "You know, that is what we're trying to get through with my dad. He thinks he can draw welfare. My mom don't want to get on welfare. I don't want to get on welfare neither."

Even though these are only expressed values, we assume that they express within certain limitations the truth as these young men see it.

From a structural point of view, they are part of America's underclass, but they are in a pathway at the present time that may yield them a productive and law-abiding life.

Interview 3

At-Risk Youths

"It kind of makes the week shorter if you miss a couple of days out of the week, and when you go back, you only have three more days, you know."

The two young men in this interview are friends. They are friends because they share common interests and like to do the same things. They also share in common that they were both present when their fathers were killed, shot in saloons. This fact may separate them from a great many students, but violence seems to be a large part of the families of at-risk youth. These boys have been selected by their assistant principal as very likely to drop out. One of the boys affirms this belief; the other says he will finish. In talking with these young men, it is our opinion that it is highly unlikely that they will finish school. They both find school boring and simply refuse to do their homework. They are not able to do work in class because they have been absent when the work was explained. Their trouble in school has involved cigarette smoking, being out of their seat, and the use of foul language. They have been taken to juvenile court for being truant but report they have had no other trouble with the law.

In regards to their families and whether or not they finished high school, Kurt's family has no high school graduates in it. His mother did not graduate from high school and works only sporadically. James' mother and his brother did not graduate, but his two sisters did.

The two respondents report that their troubles in school have centered around truancy and school rules. In contrast to the interview with persisters who see school rules for their benefit, these respondents see the school rules as unfair. As one respondent says, "I don't think the rules are fair. They always take the teacher's word over ours." He goes on to say that he got suspended for, "Well, I got suspended for saying bullshit. That's the only time I've been suspended." When asked if he thought the suspension was justified, he said, "Well, yeah, I shouldn't have said it." His reason for saying bullshit was because the teacher told him to get in his seat.

When asked what they are doing when they are out of school on suspension, they report that they stay home and watch TV. This tends to confirm what we have heard from other interviewees, that they are not out breaking the law while they are not in school. The issue of whether status offenders, such as truants, are committing crimes is a topic for another book.

The subject of peer groups and cliques arises in this interview as it did in our first interview and does in interview 4. Here the boys say that they are labelled "hoods" or "stoners" because of their long hair and how they dress. Kurt says that part of his school problems relates to an earlier peer group that he hung around with and now returns to on weekends. This peer group that exists in the housing projects is not oriented towards school. The assistant principal affirms that if they had had Kurt before he oriented around this particular peer group, he would have been a decent student, because, as the assistant principal says, he has the intellectual skills. This capable child is certainly one we hate to lose.

As far as in-groups and out-groups are concerned, the lines appear fairly drawn when Kurt says, "They don't like us, so we don't like them."

Locus of control, as has been true throughout our series of interviews, is reported as being internal. The students report the responsibility for being in trouble as their own. If they were involved with a girl who became pregnant, they report that they would be involved and support it. Marriage for them now is not in the picture. Abortion is not considered by these two young men as an option to having a baby. This is in contrast to the persisters who reported abortion as an option for them. These at-risk youth also report that when they become parents, they will be hard on their children and make them go to school. When asked if they know any pregnant girls now, they said yes. Kurt says, "Well, most of them like they have their baby, but the guys that get them pregnant, they just, you know, forget about them. They never go to see their kids or nothing." We are taken by the fact that these young men report that they would get involved with their children, but that the males they know do not get involved with their children. This type of response must make us pause and wonder about the truth as these young men can know it at this particular time.

Interview 4

Persisters

One of the key questions we are interested in addressing in this book is, are there significant differences that exist between dropouts and those who stay in school and graduate, the persisters. Characteristics that have been attributed to dropouts were discussed in Chapter 6. Among those was nonparticipation in school activities. The three persisters who were selected for this interview reported belonging to 35 organizations collectively within the school. Among the three, they reported 15, 15, and 5, respectively. This is 32 more reported activities than given by the 143 alternative school respondents collectively.

In regards to family structure, divorce, separated, etc., we might assume that there would be significant differences between those families of dropouts and those of persisters. Our research does not answer this question in a definitive way, but what goes on within the family is gleaned from some of these interviews.

When one of the persisters with very long-term goals was asked where his values came from, he said his family and that his role model was his father. He says, "You've got to have somebody to look toward and say 'He's great.'" Another student, when asked what would be her family's response if she were taken to juvenile court and charged with possession of alcohol on school grounds said, "I would probably have every privilege I've ever been given taken away from me. Well, maybe not that drastic, but my parents would be disappointed in me." This tacit support is far greater than the at-risk youth we have interviewed report getting from their family. This young lady goes on to say that, "My parents would want me to understand why what I did was wrong, and they would help me through it all." This same student, when queried about what she would do if she became pregnant, says, "I guess the first thing I would do would be to go to my mother. Because I wouldn't know where else to turn." She goes on to say that being pregnant would not be a reason to leave school. In regards to having the child or an abortion, both the female and male persisters report that they have thought about this particular dilemma, with the males being more favorable than the female toward abortion. The males state that it would not be fair to the child to bring it into the world with young, inexperienced parents. It might also be pointed out that they see the child as interfering with their goals at this point in their life. The female was more ambivalent on the subject of abortion but appears to share the same goal directions of the males.

Peer groups and cliques, which were mentioned earlier as being mechanisms of shutting out at-risk youth, is confirmed when talking with the successful persisters. As our female respondent puts it, "I am not willing to risk my position in the group by being friendly to someone new, someone I don't know." The male respondent says that his friends will walk away from him if he talks with someone who is not approved by his clique. The female respondent goes on to say, "If someone different comes in, I don't think we intentionally shut them out or anything, but we don't know them, and I don't know, a lot of times you're really afraid to go up and introduce yourself to somebody, but you're just not sure what they're going to do or anything, someone new or like you were saying, I think a lot of times maybe the people that they call themselves rednecks, I mean, I think some of it, they do bring upon themselves." A more sympathetic view in regards to how cliques shut out the outsider—in our case the at-risk youth—is expressed by one of our male respondents when he says, "It's just like apathy. You sort of just pick them out and say 'They're gonna be losers,' and they don't even get a chance to grasp any one thread of hope. They've already been labeled, and that's where cliques come in. They've got nothing to attach upon, and if the home situation is one that's deteriorating or deteriorated, then they pretty much go down." He goes on to say, "It's either up to themselves, if they can find it within themselves to bring themselves up and succeed, then that's one thing. But it's like you've got to get into a club or get a job or get some way that you feel that you're actually climbing up the ladder of success. That's the big catch. I mean, a lot of times it's the clique thing. It's a matter of economics, like the drug scene. I feel that a lot of kids sell drugs not to be evil, but it's the money. Which would you rather do? Work for $3.85 at McDonalds or make $5,000 a week selling crack?" Our female respondent goes on to make her final statement regarding peer groups when she says, "I'm where I want to be. I feel secure right now, and I wouldn't want to do anything to jeopardize it." It is most interesting to see this rejection phenomenon both by the rejecters and the rejectees.

Along the lines of peer group formation, one hears espoused from these persisters a very traditional view regarding society's mores. They report that cigarette smoking is definitely not cool. They also report that they would not associate with anyone doing drugs. When it comes to alcohol, however, this group becomes much more equivocal. It appears that they use alcohol but did not choose to brag about it. This peer groups also *knows of* girls who are pregnant but does not report personally knowing anyone who is pregnant. As one of the male respondents says, "It's not something they want to go out and publicize."

School rules are another social force that distinguish dropouts from persisters in our study. One male persister says, "Students want rules. They are for our benefit. Most of them are just for our protection and stuff?" Contrast this with what an at-risk youth says, "School rules are stupid. If I am late for class, I get suspended. If I run to class because I'm late, I'm suspended. Stupid!"

The last item we found to show strong differences between the groups is that of long-range planning and goal setting. An at-risk youth told me he didn't think he would live to be 21 years of age. A male persister had this to say about his future plans. "I've sat down and said I'm gonna be a pilot. It's going to take me four years in the academy, eight years afterwards, one year at pilot training, that's nine years. That's thirteen years altogether. I said, what do I want to do after that, because I can't be a pilot and an astronaut forever afterwards, and everybody gets old. I said, well hey, maybe I want to go into politics, maybe I want to do this. I'm already thinking ahead til I'am fifty." And, of course, these students report an internal locus of control.

Chapter 10

CHESTNUT RIDGE LEARNING CENTER: AN INNOVATIVE SOLUTION

CAROL BEILHARZ, SUZANNE ARP, REBECCA BAKER, MARY LEFLER, LINDA THOMAS, AMY WOMBLES AND PATRICIA YARNELL

During the 1990-91 school year the Loudon County, Tennessee Board of Education established a system-wide at-risk committee to examine the needs of students in danger of dropping out of school before earning their high school diplomas and to develop recommendations for addressing those needs. A year later, this committee submitted its report to the Loudon County Board of Education. Several factors were involved in the committee's recommendation including: (1) increased emphasis on providing for at-risk students; (2) rising costs involved in educating students; (3) emphasis on accountability and results instead of process; (4) encouragement to try alternatives to traditional methods; and (5) declining enrollment at the vo-tech center.

The committee recommended that (1) Loudon County Board of Education assume full administrative operation of the Loudon County Vo-Tech Center; (2) the program of half-day vocational instruction be continued for those students able to participate; (3) a full day program for students who needed a different approach to the traditional high school program be established; (4) a full day program for special education students who could benefit from vocational instruction be provided at the center, and (5) a program to reduce dropouts by providing an alternative to the traditional 180-hour per year high school credit program be instituted.

The Board of Education enthusiastically approved these recommendations and work began to have the center and its new programs in place by the Fall of 1992. The new full day program began with ninth graders and a grade was added each year until a full four year program was established in 1995. The instructional approach was to emphasize technology and practical application with academic subjects being integrated into large instructional blocks instead of the traditional single-subject per teacher method. Students would spend half their day in an academic setting and half in a vocational class. Two special education teachers were transferred from Loudon High School to provide the academic component for the resource students who could benefit from the vocational education.

A team of two academic teachers was employed each year to teach integrated (1) English and Social Studies (2) Math and Science. These teachers move through the four years of high school with their group of students in an attempt to provide continuity, security, and gradual positive attitudinal changes. The staff-designed curriculum reflects an approach intended to build on student strengths. As most students have not been successful in settings using traditional techniques and materials, alternative methods and materials are incorporated; for example, no textbooks are used except as references. Computers are used by students almost daily as are interactive video disc materials. An anonymous quote presented by one of the teachers provides a wonderful guideline: "Know your stuff, know who you are stuffing, then stuff them elegantly!" Chestnut Ridge teachers will emphatically verify that small class size is mandatory for success with these previously unsuccessful students.

Unlike traditional high school, Chestnut Ridge's grading philosophy is "no-fail." This is not to say that students cannot choose to fail, they can. However, this philosophy does allow unlimited chances to correct or make up any unacceptable or missing assignments. The idea behind this grading system is one of accountability. Students are held accountable for every assignment. No zeros are given. In order to obtain a satisfactory grade, a student must have completed all assignments to a minimum level of 80 percent. This system forces each student to have exposure to each skill taught. Because students can "make up" missed work at full credit, they are more likely to complete any missed assignments than they would be in a traditional grading system. Also, because students are held accountable for each and every assignment, teachers seem more willing to give full credit for all completed assignments.

The idea of being able to "gain forgiveness for past mistakes" is very attractive to students. They tend, once they fully understand the grading system, to not give up on themselves. One example of this is a student named Tijuana.

This sixteen-year-old freshman transferred into Chestnut Ridge from a traditional high school two weeks into the first grading period. As a repeat freshman, she had attended three high schools prior to Chestnut Ridge. Her attitude was defiant from the first day. She refused to do any of her assignments or take part in any activities declaring that she would "just take a zero." After three weeks of school and watching other students work and gain full "forgiveness" for late work, Tijuana began to see that she, too, could be successful. She approached her teachers about making up her work. Tijuana did go on to complete each and every assignment that had been given during the six week grading period. She completed her freshman year doing work that was above the satisfactory level and turned it in on a timely basis.

The grading philosophy at Chestnut Ridge is not traditional. It does not penalize students for late work or reward them with passing grades for "D" level work. Instead, it seeks to teach the "at-risk" students that they are accountable for all work. It does not take long for the students to realize that it is better to do their work, and do it well, the first time around.

What has been described thus far is loosely referred to as the "regular" academic program. Some students who come to Chestnut Ridge, usually after one or two unsuccessful years at another high school, do not fit into these classes. They have credit or course needs that must be met, or they exhibit behaviors which prevent them and students around them from being successful. Although these two academic classrooms have been renamed several times, they are probably most often and accurately referred to as the *Alternative Program.* The structure of this program is a self-contained classroom with one teacher. Each student has an individualized program designed for his or her particular course requirement needs. Students are required to complete assignments for the classes they are taking and to work independently with teacher supervision. Oftentimes, students who do not perform well in the computer-based programs will excel in the Alternative Program. An excellent example is Brandon who failed to complete his ninth grade work and was placed in this program for a year.

During his time, Brandon was to finish his ninth grade work and earn his tenth grade credits. He successfully completed all work for both grades and at the beginning of his eleventh grade year, Brandon chose to stay in the Alternative program; he had found his "niche."

Since 1991, the Alternative Program has graduated 125 students.

The vocational class offerings vary from year to year. Offerings include, at least ten at any one time, from the following: Auto Body, Auto Mechanics, Graphic Arts, Cosmetology, Child Care, Office Occupations, Commercial Food Service, Welding, Machine Shop, Commercial Cleaning, Building Trades, Building and Grounds Maintenance, Horticulture, and our newest, Health Occupations. A primary goal of the whole program, both the academic and vocational components, is to prepare students to be productive and dependable employees upon high school graduation, and to be ready to attend further vocational training. Every attempt is made to utilize the skills being learned to improve the campus and program. Some examples include:

- Commercial Cleaning students help clean the building.
- Commercial Foods students help prepare the lunches and clean up.
- Auto Mechanics students work on student and staff vehicles.
- Those in Cosmetology do inexpensive haircuts for all.
- Child care has a free nursery so that students with babies can continue their education in addition to learning how to care for their infants.
- Office Occupations students do word processing chores for teachers.
- The Graphic Arts Department does printing for many community agencies.
- The Building Trades class has added needed spaces onto the building including a lunch/all purpose room and a health clinic.
- Students have helped with landscaping, mowing, and general outdoor cleanup.
- The Health Occupations students are kept busy monitoring the blood pressure of some "stressed-out" staff.

Much effort is put into students having a successful job placement experience in the senior year. Ideally, they work in their chosen vocational area and can continue this job after graduation. Nothing they are told in class seems to duplicate this real world experience which involves making money and losing a job because of absenteeism, tardiness, or lack of productivity.

The Counseling Program at Chestnut Ridge:
Focusing on What Is Unique

It is taken for granted that all the traditional areas of a counseling program such as handling incoming and outgoing students records, personal crises, social interactions, informational presentation, post high school educational and career needs are handled in the most professional manner. It is appropriate then to now examine more closely what is done differently at Chestnut Ridge to try to meet the unusual needs of our at-risk population which is a majority of the students rather that the minority that comprises the student body at a typical public high school.

With regular high school diplomas in hand, Chestnut Ridge students are prepared to continue their education at the Junior Colleges in Tennessee; about 8 percent choose this route, although not all immediately after graduation. There is much emphasis on students being totally familiar with the ten or so areas of concentration offered by the Tennessee Technology Centers; typically these programs last from six months to two years. Loudon County is conveniently located in the middle of three of these, each a 30-minute commute. Representatives of each of these three centers–Knoxville, Harriman, and Athens–come to address the Seniors during the Fall semester. These presentations are followed by a visit and tour within a two week period. Chestnut Ridge graduates are very well-prepared to continue their education and training at these centers immediately after graduation. All those interested are encouraged and helped through the application process. Chestnut Ridge offers some financial aid from a scholarship fund to those students who pursue vo-tech education.

Despite this concentration effort, the majority of Chestnut Ridge graduates are still more interested in going straight to work and of course, making as much money as possible! The needs of business and industry in the area are constantly being assessed in an effort to provide superior employees for them. The counselor and job placement coordinator at Chestnut Ridge participate actively on the Chamber of Commerce "Educational Excellence" committee which focuses on presenting interesting, energetic programs to Loudon County's ninth graders in an attempt to make them more cognizant of what industry looks for in an employee and what an employee needs in his or her job. Frequently, interested students visit local businesses and industries. In half day vocational classes, students are constantly exposed to what is expected of them on the job. By the time they are Seniors, many students are in supervised work experiences in place of vocational classes. This has been a brief overview of post-high school goals for Chestnut Ridge students, but it is important to look at what is done before consideration of post-high school and career concentrations.

It is no surprise to educators that school attendance dramatically correlates with achievement and that Chestnut Ridge's incoming students are below average in academic achievement and above average for school absences. Some of this may be attributable to higher incidences of illness but the larger factor seems to be that many of the students' parents do not consider regular school attendance to have great value. Some have had negative school experiences both as students and as parents of students. Often, by the time they are in high school, Chestnut Ridge students are pretty much in charge of their own lives because their parents are unable to parent, or are distracted by other younger children, or by their own pressing life problems.

Loudon County Schools and the Juvenile Justice System initiated the Truancy Board four years ago. It is comprised of several school, community agency, and juvenile court representatives. When a student has excessive absences, usually around ten (each school determines which of its students would benefit from this experience), the student and parent are summoned to appear before the board. Typically, the family's case is heard, recommendations for assistance are made, and a contract is written and signed by the board members and the family. It stipulates that any future absences or tardies must be supported by a doctor's excuse or the student will be summoned to appear in front of the judge in juvenile court. This has served as a fairly effective deterrent for many students. In addition to this, it became necessary to positively reinforce school attendance in an attempt to teach students what employers feel is the most important employee behavior—coming to work every day and on time. Various incentives have been used the last four years including cash, outside school parties, field trips to game and entertainment centers, end of year trips to Dollywood, various coupons, drawings for televisions, novelty telephones, compact disc players, tickets, anything else affordable or donated! Currently, activities and incentives which seem to work well and are among the easier to administrate are being used. Three weeks of perfect attendance earn students a ticket out of class for a 10-15 minute break with free soft drink, juice, or candy bar. Six weeks brings the break and a day out of school without being counted absent (this mimics earned vacation days in the workplace), and frequently, a sandwich or french fries coupon is given. In addition to these incentives, a drawing is held and a fairly nice prize is given at the end of each semester for those students who have had perfect attendance. The increase in attendance the first year was dramatic but seems to have stabilized at present. Students are often heard saying, "I can't miss because I'll mess up my perfect attendance," "When do we get our break," and "When is our free day out?"

This program was designed for those students needing something the regular high schools could not deliver. Students come from five different middle schools. Many students who are struggling at their regular high schools transfer between semesters to Chestnut Ridge, and most students who move into our county midsemester are encouraged to attend Chestnut Ridge. It became apparent that even this flexibility could not satisfy the needs of the 16 and 17 year-olds who arrived with no or minimal high school credits. These students were often bright and could learn but had not been motivated enough to earn passing grades and credits. The counselors became aware of an in-school GED program which had been in place in other states and in two schools in Tennessee. Application was made and Chestnut Ridge was approved as the third G.E.D. Exit Option + 2 program in the state.

> Ronnie was in our first class; the shy, barely 17-year-old was practically dragged into our building by his older girlfriend in December. He had been out of school in another state for a couple of years, living where he could find a place. His search for his other parent brought him to Tennessee. The last records we could get were a less than sterling half of seventh grade. He had to get up before 6:00 a. m. each morning to make all the connections to get to school but he liked our Commercial Foods program (many of his pick-up jobs had been in food service) and he was really motivated to earn his GED. Ronnie defied the odds, making huge gains by the end of April, and became one of our first three to pass the GED test.

A brief profile of the students may be interesting; these results were anonymously self-reported but it is felt they are quite accurate. Approximately 40 percent are on free or reduced lunch, although more would probably qualify, 40 percent are identified as handicapped—mostly LD, 40 percent have appeared in juvenile court, 40 percent drink alcohol, half have used illegal drugs, two-thirds are sexually active, and 4 percent are parents or soon to be. (This figure is much lower than previous years; there is hope that it is being impacted in a positive way.)

Probably one of the most effective activities of the counselor is networking with every outside agency that may have some service to offer any of the students. Two of the four initiatives of the Loudon County Health Improvement Council target Chestnut Ridge students; the first is Adolescent Pregnancy Prevention. The county students who are parents or fit the profile of becoming a parent before what "enlightened adults" in society think is desirable, are likely to be found among this same population of at-risk students. Elementary counselors and teachers profess the ability to identify these children—especially the girls—by 4th or 5th grade. "Baby-Think-It-Over," the very lifelike doll that demands to be held, cared for, and fed is utilized. It provides very realistic sleep deprivation by crying loudly until its needs are met. Teen moms present what it is REALLY like to be there—alone at home with the baby. Several class presentations are done by agencies supporting abstinence only and by those who believe if students are not going to abstain, they must know how to properly use birth control and be introduced to other risks they are taking. It is hoped that these efforts are impacting students; pregnancy numbers are much lower this year.

The second council initiative that is so important is teaching effective parenting. Teen parents are required to take an excellent vocational class on child care and parenting where they learn and are supervised in the Daycare Center. School is still a reasonable requirement for student parents because of the in-school nursery for their babies. A strong parent education and support group, "Parent Project," has been started at Chestnut Ridge. It was designed by parents for parents of difficult to manage and even out of control adolescents. Led by four trained facilitators, the classes are three hours long, meeting once a week for 10 weeks. Participant reviews have been excellent.

"Healthy Families" is a grant project from Helen Ross McNabb Center which targets pregnant girls and assists them with all their needs including health care, parenting skills, and clothing. Aid is continued after delivery, even until the child is five years-old, if necessary. An interesting phenomena here is that it is not unusual for the girls to turn this service down, family members are often suspicious that "those people" will take the baby away from them.

Not unlike adolescent girls everywhere, some students get pregnant from a relationship with an older male. The school interacts a great deal with the Sexual Assault Crisis Center. Their counselors do small group presentations, then discussion groups, and frequently, individual counseling with victims. Raising students' awareness of what harassment, abuse, assault, and rape are will, hopefully, prevent some of them from becoming victims in the future.

Another area of concern can be found in the high incidence of alcohol and drug use. A local treatment facility has provided a program director to do group presentations and individual treatment needs assessments. Also, in conjunction with the "parent project," one Chestnut Ridge teacher who was formerly a treatment facility counselor, is working with the adolescents while the parents are in class. A contract with another treatment facility provided a student assistance program counselor who came in one day a week to work with referred students. The success of this type program is almost totally dependent on the qualifications and abilities of that individual counselor. Yet another agency provided a facilitator for a very successful adventure-based counseling group, a really great experience for a few students who had difficulty working with peers.

Grants have become such a necessary source of program monies in the ninetys. Through a grant, a juvenile court probation officer has come into school once a week to do group counseling with assigned students. The Chestnut Ridge counselor participated in the research and writing for a grant that focuses on a clinic and thorough health care in the schools. The grant was awarded and work on implementation is under way. The staff is always attentive to those resources or grants which may help address pressing needs such as alcohol, drug, and tobacco use prevention, and conflict resolution.

Other agencies not previously mentioned with whom Chestnut Ridge works closely include: Department of Children's Services (abuse and neglect issues and the new welfare reform act, "Families First"); Roane State Community College and J.T.P.A. (adult education and further job training); the Health Department (especially concerning pregnancy testing and sexually transmitted diseases); support groups such as A.A., N.A., Alateen, and Grief Recovery; the Legal Aid Society; and two local family resource centers to name a few. Hiwassee College has provided "Upward Bound" for six students who are first generation college bound but do not have the necessary resources and support to pursue this appropriate goal. The experiences and needed individual support have been invaluable to these students. Hopefully, the opportunity to participate in this program will be ongoing for students who need additional assistance to attend college.

Several counselor training programs at the University of Tennessee have found Chestnut Ridge to be very "intern and practicum student friendly." Chestnut Ridge has an endless supply of high school age candidates interested in working in the U.T. students assigned areas such as: goal setting, reality therapy, decision making, and anger management.

Fine arts experiences are not commonly found under the counseling program domain, but it became apparent that if these students did not have their first theater experience here, they may never have it. These efforts have resulted in almost our entire student body seeing quality productions of "To Kill a Mockingbird," "Christy," and "Camelot." Many others have chosen to go in a group to an opera, a ballet, and dress rehearsals for presentations by a local theater group, "The Tellico Village Players," whose members have been extremely supportive of Chestnut Ridge in one of its most unusual programs, which follows.

During the program's first year, eight retired individuals, who had moved into a newly developed area on the water in Loudon County, wanted to contribute some time to a worthwhile project and were easily convinced that Chestnut Ridge met those requirements. They provided unusual activities for students such as bowling, needlework, crafts, painting, and jewelry making. This mentor/tutor program has evolved over the last three years to include 55-60 adults and 175-200 adolescents. Currently, there are 35 very active mentors and around 65 students who are directly involved with one of these very talented, energetic individuals. One mentor in particular has been instrumental in starting an "interview loan closet" filled with donated, neatly organized clothes which would be appropriate for students to wear to a job interview. Frequently, students do not have "nice" clothes. She then organized a pre-Christmas giveaway of the leftover donations. She has enlisted friends to come in to do mock interviews with the seniors and to give lively class programs on how to present themselves. She has taken a group of girls to a friend's dress shop for an inside look at the business and obtained opera and ballet tickets. Three of the mentors have provided arts and crafts experiences for about ten talented students.   The mentors prefer to serve six but do not turn away the interested students who keep sitting in rather than passing by!   Mentors have taken students out to lunch, to a museum, to libraries, movies, shopping, to a one-time job, to get a picture I.D., then on to register for a G.E.D. test.   One mentor helped students weld beautiful lawn art in the school shop which she sold to neighbors and friends for $35 to $60 each to support the drafts program. Two mentors have closely-knit small groups of 3 - 6 students each who often just sit and talk, play a game, or do a project. Every Wednesday, Ray comes to the counseling office door and asks, "Is my mentor coming today?" (She always does!) Another of the adults has taught his trade, upholstery, to two interested boys. Yet another has taught his boys various carpentry skills while contributing to the needs of the school with shelves in offices, the loan closet, and a small library. After two years, it would be difficult to convince him that there are other students who might work ALMOST as well as his helper and student, Sam.   Yet another gentleman comes into the machine shop one or two mornings a week to work on machining projects with a small group of students. As least half of the mentors and students are most interested in and comfortable with working on specific objectives from the Tennessee Competency Test which students need to learn in order to pass the test and get a regular high school diploma. The tutors are MUCH more impatient with the slowness in state scoring and returning the results than the students and teachers. They take great pride and joy in their students passing or even improving their scores. This often happens in the students' Senior year when they are REALLY serious about learning all the material; a victory for all!

An absolute necessity for a program such as Chestnut Ridge's to be successful is an energetic staff whose members are willing to constantly evaluate, be flexible, be open to changes and adjustments in curriculum and structure, and who are willing to commit to the idea that every child has value and can become a contributing member of his or her community.

Chestnut Ridge Learning Center's success can best be summed up by two students' unsolicited statements concerning what this new program meant to them. The first said, "At my other school, I dreaded getting up in the morning and going to school, but here I don't dread getting up in the morning to come. I can't wait to get here." The other student expressed these feelings somewhat emotionally, "This school kept me from dropping out. How many other freshmen do you know who are almost 18? I can make it now." Chestnut

Ridge Learning Center has made a tremendous difference in the lives of these two young people and from observations, a number of other students at this center have also benefited tremendously from this new program.(1)

Chapter 11

MIGRANTS AND SEASONAL FARM WORKERS

It's a mighty hard row that my pore hands have hoed,
My pore feet have traveled a hot dusty road,
Out of your dustbowl and westward we rolled,
Your deserts was hot and your mountains was cold.

I've worked in your orchards of peaches and prunes,
I've slept on the ground by the light of your moon,
At the edge of your city you will find us and then
We come with the dust and we're gone with the wind.

California and Arizona, I've worked all your crops,
And it's North up to Oregon to gather your hops,
Dig beets from your ground, cut the grapes from your vine
To place on your table your light sparkling wine.

Green pastures of plenty from dry desert ground,
From that Grand Coulee dam where the water runs down,
Every state in this union us migrants have been
And we'll work in this fight and we'll fight 'til we win.

Oh, it's always we rambled, your river and I,
All along your green valley I'll work 'til I die,
My land I'll defend with my life need it be,
Green pastures of plenty must always be free!*

One of the more intriguing groups as described above by Woodie Guthrie to be examined when considering the topic of at-risk youth, dropouts, or pushouts is the migrant. Migrant families were described eloquently by Michael Harrington (1963) as America's invisible poor.

Robert Coles (1967) wrote poignantly about this group of people in his classic *Migrants, Sharecroppers, and Mountaineers.* Coles's work of two decades ago, written in an ethnographic style, ushers the reader into the daily life of the migrant living in the Appalachian South. Coles discovered that school attendance of many Appalachian migrant youth is deter-

---

*From Woodrow Wilson Guthrie, "Pastures of Plenty," Harrington, 1963, p. 51.

mined by the amount of clothing to go around. Coles (1967) found that oftentimes there simply were not enough clothes to go around, so children would go to school depending upon who had the appropriate clothing. This was only one factor in who would attend school, but obviously an important one. Coles (1967) also reported that migrant youth tended not to go to school because they felt that teachers had a negative image of them and did not respect what they knew. This lack of respect by the teachers of what the migrant student knew was a strong force in alienating the child from school.

Eliot Wigginton (1972) and his *Foxfire* series has done a great deal to emphasize the importance of what the Appalachian people, including migrants, know. He, possibly more than anyone else, has presented the value of Appalachian culture in contemporary America. It seems a shame that some teachers were incapable of discovering the importance of what migrant youth know.

Harrington (1963), in his description of migrants as the invisible poor, states: "No one knows exactly how many migrants there are. The government takes census of migrant birds, but not of migrant human beings" (p. 57). In recent years, however, quite a few people have become aware of migrant workers.

Migrant children are dramatically deprived. They work in the fields even though there are laws against it. Among the Texas Mexicans, the educational average is six years of schooling, and the chances are that it was received on the fly, that it was constantly interrupted, and that it was inferior (Harrington, 1963).

If anything can be ascribed to the migrant in America, it is that he or she is powerless. Because of their constant movement, the migrant is part of no political constituency and has no political base. Obviously, education for his or her children has not been a top priority in America.

Coles (1967) becomes more detailed and specific when he speaks of migrant children thusly; "Space, time, and movement, to become conceptual, mean very special things to a migrant child and so does food, which can never be taken for granted" (p. 63). Coles (1967) states:

> Many of the children I have studied these past years in various parts of Florida and all along the eastern seaboard view life as a constant series of trips, undertaken rather desperately in a seemingly endless expanse of time. Those same children are both active and fearful, full of initiative and desperately forlorn, driven to a wide range of ingenious and resourceful deeds, and terribly paralyzed by all sorts of things: the

weakness and lethargy that go with hunger and malnutrition, and the sadness and hopelessness that I suppose can be called part of their preschool education . . . these children state how foolish it is to spend a week in school and another few days there and then a couple of weeks up yonder. (P. 63.)

By definition, life for migrants is a matter of travel and movement, and their children soon enough get to know that fact which means they get to feel tentative about people, places, and things.

Time and space are obviously central forces in the life of migrant children. They never seem to know exactly where they will be and for how long. As they state, in this framework of living where so much that is important to them is unknown, school is foolish. These factors set the cultural tone that forms the basis for the migrant child's approach to education and schooling. From the very beginning, barriers are in place that keep the migrant child out of school and cause him or her to be an early school leaver. Migrant children see everything as temporary. Places come and go, along with people and schools and fellow friends. The term dropout may not be appropriate when discussing migrant children, as they are not in school long enough oftentimes to be considered dropouts.

As one of Coles's (1967) respondents states: "A good school is one where the teacher is friendly and she wants to be on your side, and she'll ask you to tell the other kids some of the things you can do and all you've done, you know, about the crops and like that" (p. 72). On the other hand, many migrant children report leaving school, sometimes sadly, sometimes happily, because they have been ignored or even scorned.

As another of Coles's (1967) respondents stated: "If you don't finish school you'll have nothing to do and you'll starve to death so it's best to go to school, even if you don't like to" (p. 71). For the migrant child, the schoolhouse is a mixed bag and an enterprise that catches him or her with mixed emotions. "First you have to stay alive then comes school" (p. 71), according to one of Coles's (1967) respondents.

A further description of the migrant family's view of the school is presented in this quote:

If you drove in your car for miles around, my children could show you every bird's nest there is here, and where they're all living, the animals. They keep their eyes on the crops, too. The foreman will always ask them how is everything doing, just like he'll ask me or my husband,

and I do believe the children know better than we do. That's why they hate to go over to that school. They'll be setting the whole day, and the teacher will be pushing things on them, the letters and the numbers like that, and she'll call them the same things the white people do, just as bad and they'll come home and say they are *dumb* — for going over there and listening to her. They tell me they'd rather go out and listen to the animals make noise and help their daddy, if they can, and keep themselves busy and not bother me, than go off there to school and be told all the time that the colored people are no good, and they'll always be like that, because we're working on the land and we're so poor and we don't know how to be clean with ourselves and behave the way we should. (P. 189.)

It should come as no surprise that the migrant, beset with all of his/her problems at home, hunger, lack of clothes, and little or no money, would not want to go to school to face the many harassments aimed directly at them by schools and the teacher.

Coles (1967) states that migrant children often learn to live with an almost uncanny mixture of realism and mysticism. Many of them retreat to a private life where school means nothing, is often forsaken completely, even the pretense of going. Their cycles of development are not the same as other children either. Whereas migrant children may be energetic at age five, by age ten they become sullen and tired. In the older children, however, there appears to be an identification of purpose with their parents, that purpose being one of survival. Sadly, they feel worthless, blamed, frowned upon, and spoken ill of.

An interesting case to illustrate this point on migrant children is that of Jeannette, in Jones County, North Carolina. Coles (1967) describes her in his chapter entitled "Stranded Children." Coles (1967) states: "Eventually I had to face the fact that a girl I initially considered distinctly retarded turned out to be perhaps the brightest of all the so-called stranded children I am now trying to describe — children whose fathers like Jeanette's still work as sharecroppers, tenant farmers, or field hands" (p. 171). Her behaviors, as described by Coles (1967), would not generally be well received in a traditional public school classroom. Coles (1967) describes her as full of imagination and wonder and humor but also confusion and gloom. Coles (1967) states: "Perhaps it was my own nervousness that made me pin words like 'retarded,' 'inappropriate' or 'eccentric' on a girl's open and direct curiosity" (p. 171). One can only imagine how often these types of mistakes are made regarding school children who are different, especially those who come from a culture like that of the migrant.

To illustrate the differences between migrant children, whether hidden, stranded, or uprooted, Coles (1967) compared them to urban children and, based on drawings Coles had them do, found that the rural migrant child tended to see him or herself as part of something larger than himself. The urban child tended to draw him or herself more than the migrant child did. Coles implies that the urban child focuses on self more than the rural migrant child does.

Hargis, in Chapter 4, evokes the virtue of the one-room schoolhouse and the individualization of instruction that he terms curriculum-based assessment. Here is what one of Coles's subjects has to say about one-room schools and their eventual demise:

> The teacher says we'll have big buildings, and they'll be made of brick and have a lot of rooms and we'll be coming from all over, way far off, to the school, just like they do for high school. She said she wasn't sure all schools like ours would disappear, though. She said a lot of us really like them and are used to them, and it's hard to move too far because of the mountains. I'd miss the older children, I would, if we only studied with each other. (P. 254.)

In this school, the older children help in teaching the younger children, and cooperative learning appears to work. With the passage of time, 22 years since Coles's work, these schools described by Coles have eventually disappeared. Hargis calls for a revival of their beneficial qualities.

In concluding this section on the cultural background of migrants, sharecroppers, and mountaineers, the following quote sums up the feeling Coles (1967) has of them: "Those Appalachian parents certainly do take notice of their children's suffering, for one reason because they are parents, and for another, because they are traditionally proud and defiant people" (p. 264). Coles (1967) makes explicitly clear that there are differences between the three groups, with mountaineers being somewhat better off than migrants or sharecroppers. Our focus in this chapter is on migrant youth who leave school early, and it is to them that we now move.

High School Equivalency Program/
College Assistance Migrant Program

In 1966, two programs under federal aegis were established to help migrant and seasonal farm worker children stay in school and complete a general education degree and then possibly to go on to college. These programs are called the High School Equivalency Program (HEP) and the College Assistance Migrant Program (CAMP). A discussion of these two programs, designed to reduce migrant and seasonal farm worker dropouts, follows.

The High School Equivalency Program (HEP) was created in 1967 by Noel Klores and Ruth Groves, administrators of the Office of Economic Opportunity (OEO) for migrants and seasonal farm workers. Their intent was to implement a program that would provide farm worker youth with an experience which would have economic opportunity payoffs. A pilot project was started at Catholic University in Washington, D.C. Four years later, the College Assistance Migrant Program (CAMP) was started.

HEP and CAMP have been serving the migrants and seasonal farm workers' community since the mid-1960s. With an average of 3,000 students being served each year, these programs have directly impacted the lives of over 45,000 individuals, offering them an alternative to the unending cycle of poverty and illiteracy found too often within the migrant and seasonal farm worker population.

HEPs and CAMPs are currently funded on an annual basis and administered through the United States Department of Education Office of Migrant Education. These programs are geographically distributed within fourteen states and Puerto Rico.

The following legislative history elucidates the evolvement of legislation mandating services for migrant and seasonal farm worker children.

1. Title I, Public Law 89-10 ESEA, 1965 provided federal support for education programs for disadvantaged children. The migratory children of migratory agricultural workers were not specifically identified in the disadvantaged population to be served.
2. Public Law 89-750, Education Amendments of 1966, incorporated special provisions for migratory children of migratory agricultural workers, provided for SEA grant monies to be used for interstate coordination of migrant education program activities.
3. Public Law 90-247, Education Amendments of 1967, provided for

the eligibility of formerly migratory children for migrant education program services.

4. Public Law 91-230, Education Amendment of 1969, provided for grants for migratory children based on the number to be served; for reallocation of excess funds; and for use of carryover funds (Tydings Amendment).

5. Public Law 92-318, Education Amendments of 1972, provided for eligibility and services to meet the special educational needs of preschool migratory children of migratory agricultural workers; established the priority of currently migratory children; required evaluation to assess effectiveness and review of States' administration and report the findings and recommendations for improvement to Congress by December 31, 1973.

6. Public Law 93-380, Education Amendments of 1974, provided for the eligibility of migratory children of migratory fishers; established the 40-80-120 percent funding formula to be based on the established number of migratory children and for this formula to be based on the established number of migratory children and for this purpose to use statistics made available by the Migrant Student Record Transfer System (MSRTS) or some other system deemed by the commissioner to be more accurate.

7. First migrant education program specific regulations, 45 CFR 116, incorporating all statutory requirements from 1965 to 1974, were published in the Federal Register, July 13, 1977.

8. Public Law 95-561, Education Amendment of 1978, provided for adjustments in the numbers of migratory children to reflect the additional costs of operating summer school programs; required parental advisory councils at the State and local levels; established the "By-Pass Provision" authority to be used by the Commissioner if a State is unable or unwilling to conduct a program; and established a specific 5 percent set-aside for the coordination of migrant education program coordination activities.

9. Second migrant education program specific regulations, 45 CFR 116d, incorporating statutory requirements in Public Law 95-561, published in the Federal Register April 3, 1980.

10. Public Law 97-35, Education Consolidation and Improvement Act of 1981, continued authorization of the Chapter 1 programs including the program for migratory children.

11. Technical Amendments to ECIA Public Law 98-211 (December 8, 1983) and Public Law 98-312 (June 12, 1984) provided:

    • Eligibility for migratory children of migratory fishers residing and moving in the geographically largest school areas, specifically the 18,000 square miles (or more) school districts in Alaska, and that fishing as the principal means of personal subsistence as well as commercial fishing may be a qualifying migratory activity.

    • Clarification of the applicability of Chapter 1 provisions on the following to the migrant program:

        a. parental participation
        b. fiscal requirements
        c. maintenance of effort
        d. sufficient size, scope, and quality of projects
        e. definitions
        f. SEA eligibility
        g. service to preschool children
        h. application content
        i. evaluation

12. Third migrant education program specific regulations, 34 CFR Par 201, 204 incorporating statutory requirements of Public Law 97-35, Public Law 98-211, and Public Law 98-312, published in the Federal Register April 30, 1985.

13. Public Law 99-159, National Science Foundation Authorization Act for Fiscal Year 1986, amended Section 143 (Interstate and Intrastate Coordination of Migrant Education Activities) by taking out the provision for "grants" and only leaving the provision for entering into "contract" with SEAs.

    It also provided that the MSRTS contract continue to be awarded to the SEA receiving the award the previous year, unless a majority of the states notify the secretary in writing that such agency has substantially failed to perform its responsibilities under the contract for the previous year.

    The section also included that for purposes of federal law the MSRTS shall not be considered a federal system of records.

Along with the legislative history of migrant education, there grew a movement that established a set of national goals for migrant education. These goals included:

1. Specifically designed curricular programs in academic disciplines based upon migrant children's assessed needs;

2. Success-oriented academic programs, career options and counseling activities, and vocational skill training that encourages migrant children's retention in school and contributes to success in later life;

3. Communication skills programs which reflect migrant children's linguistic and cultural backgrounds;

4. Supportive services that foster physical and mental well-being for migrant children's successful participation in the basic instructional programs, including dental, medical, nutritional, and psychological services;

5. Programs developed through interagency coordination at the federal, state, and local levels;

6. A component for meaningful migrant parent involvement in the education of their children and in which the cooperative efforts of parents and educators will be directed toward the improvement of migrant children's academic and social skills;

7. Staff development opportunities that increase staff competencies in the cognitive, psychomotor, and affective domains;

8. A component to identify and enroll all eligible migrant children;

9. Preschool and kindergarten programs designed to meet migrant children's developmental needs and prepare them for future success;

10. Development, evaluation, and dissemination of information designed to increase knowledge of program intent, intra- and interstate program development, the contribution of migrants to the community, and the overall effect of the program; and

11. The assurance that sequence and continuity will be an inherent part of the migrant child's education program through a system which facilitates the exchange of methods, concepts, and materials, and the effective use of the Migrant Student Record Transfer System in the exchange of the student records.

Through this development of national goals of migrant education evolved two other organizations along with HEP and CAMP that were designed to provide continuity in the education of migrant and seasonal farm worker children and to ease the dropout rate among these children. These programs are the Migrant Student Record Transfer System (MSRTS) and the National Association of State Directors of Migrant Education (NASDME). These two groups, MSRTS and NASDME, have designed an appropriate student record and the carrier system to transfer these records as the migratory student moves about the country. In 1975, the data base reflected 630,263 students on file; by 1982 the records showed 1,500,000, but no one knows how many migrant students there are (Federal Aid Report, 1982). These numbers reflect the need to develop and implement programs such as HEP and CAMP to meet the educational and social needs of migrant and seasonal farm worker children. The following quote from a Maryland school superintendent summarizes the situation as it reflects schooling in the 1980s.

> As we have carried forth our grand experiment in universal free public education, we have largely fashioned a system that serves well those who are white, middle to upper income, well motivated, and from relatively stable families. As students have deviated more and more from that norm the system has served them less and less well. The critical mass of at-risk children and youth has grown so large that it now threatens the entire system. Instead of blaming the students for not fitting the system we must restructure the system to provide appropriate educational services to those at risk. (Jibrell, 1987, p. 2.)

This quote obviously reflects several important things going on in American education. One is that by the beginning of the twenty-first century, the majority of students in the public school classroom will be non-white, and secondly, as has been argued cogently throughout this text, a change in the system is certainly in need.

The importance of the need for programs aimed at reducing the migrant and seasonal farm worker dropout rate is illustrated in a statement by a former Health, Education, and Welfare (HEW) now Health and Human Services secretary when he said "Children of migrant agricultural workers are the most educationally deprived group of children in our nation" (Celebreeze, 1982, p. 1). They enter school late. Their attendance is poor. Their illiteracy is high.

Studies indicate that most migrant children are far below grade level, and their ultimate school achievement is usually fourth grade (Celebreeze, 1982). By 1982, the United States Department of Education reported that 9 out of 10 migrant children never enter high school, and only 3 of 10 of those who do enter ever graduate. In 1985, Johnson et al. reported that the dropout rates for migrant students are obviously far higher than for the rest of the public school population. Problems specific to migrant dropout rates include, according to Johnson et al. (1985), when first enrolling in school, migrant children are frequently placed in a lower grade than is appropriate for their age. In subsequent years, migrant children are often retained for reasons such as size, maturity, or language limitations. Being overage is presently the highest predictor of dropout behavior among migrant students. Most migrant students who are two years overage drop out before graduation. (Being overage is a good predictor of dropping out for all students.) Other problem areas for migrants in graduating from high school include: credit deficiency, inadequate knowledge of school requirements, proficiency exams, and lack of acceptance. This lack of acceptance by non-migrant students leads to less participation in school activities by the migrant student, which leads to just another reason not to attend school. This non-acceptance process is described earlier in this chapter in the material presented by Coles (1967). The authors, in Chapter 6, discuss the importance of involvement in school activities as a hedge on dropping out.

A further need to initiate programs for migrant children through the migrant educational program was cited by Bertoglio in 1985. He claimed that:

1. Migrant students had a high incidence of mobility.
2. They were looked upon by school districts as non-residence children and, as such, not their responsibility.
3. The regular school year did not accommodate short span units of instruction for limited-attendance, non-resident migrant students.
4. There was no continuity of instruction from school district to school district, much less from state to state as the students migrated.
5. There were no records nor means by which to transfer academic and health information while the migrant students are on the move. In addition, there was no system for the transfer of secondary school credits for accrual to meet graduation requirements.
6. There was a need to take into consideration the erratic cycle of agricultural activity and subsequent school attendance into determining the entitlement entity.

Following the lead of Bertoglio (1985), Congressman William D. Ford (1988) stated:

Understanding the migrant situation involves knowing his or her circumstance. They drop out of school at a rate almost unparalleled by any other group in the country. The resulting lack of academic credentials leads them into a life cycle characterized by migration, low status jobs, frequent unemployment, and low wages. (P. 2.)

Jibrell (1987), continuing in this line of thought, told the National Governor's Association that the inability to display basic skills, combined with poverty and/or minority group membership, is the deadly combination that leads to dropping out among migrant children.

This concludes the section on background information regarding migrant and seasonal farm worker children along with programs designed to meet the needs of these students over the past 20-some-odd years. What now follows is an interview with a migrant farm worker involved in the College Assistance Migrant Program (CAMP) at The University of Tennessee in Knoxville, Tennessee. Much of what he has to say does not support the material found in *Migrants, Sharecroppers, and Mountaineers* (1967). It may be that our subject is not typical of the migrant families Coles (1967) studied or that migrant families have changed since the time of Coles's research.

It is important to note, however, that the subject sees himself as a migrant and reports that he was viewed by others as a migrant, especially his teachers, while he was growing up in Alabama. He reports that not as much was made of his migrant status in New York, where he and his family picked apples, cherries, and pears, because there were so many other migrant families around. He says, "The only way that they would know that we were migrants is either we'd tell them or they'd see us out in the fields. Other than that, they would not know because of the way we dress and the way we carry ourselves. The way we talk, they would not think we are migrant or seasonal farm workers. And that's both in Alabama as well as in New York." He goes on to say that others tend to feel that migrants live with only a limited life status position of poverty. He says, "Because we're migrants, because we have a decent home and we have nice cars, people think that we're doing something illegal."

Our subject, Kenneth, is one of eight children. All of the siblings have graduated from high school, with the exception of the youngest, who is still in school. Kenneth's parents did not graduate from high school; his mother quit in the ninth grade and his father in the sixth. Kenneth says, however, "They just always felt that it was very important, because, you know, they didn't have it, they just always stressed education, they forced us to go." Kenneth points out that his family did not follow the crops like many migrant families do, and that he did his field work after school and on weekends. It was during the summer that the family migrated to New York State to pick fruit.

Coles (1967) describes the gaiety of early childhood of migrant children and how that ends so soon. When asked to recollect about his earliest remembrances in the fields, Kenneth says, "At first, it was just like a little game, you know, cause like I attended school in the morning, got out at 2:30, go home, change clothes, and we'd go to the fields. But all I did, you know, was goofed off at that time, until I became of age and really knew what it was all about, you know, I became of some value to the family. I guess you could say I really didn't have any idea til I became a little older."

Even though Kenneth does not fit the mold described by Coles (1967), he does see himself as a migrant and reports that his teachers viewed him as a migrant. He says, "Yes, we were known as migrant students. By mostly the teachers, that is." It is reported that teachers often put down migrant students and seldom play on their positive contributions. Kenneth says he did not experience a great many put-downs and did have some positive experiences while he was in school, but these were not related to his migrant status. His positive school experiences probably grew out of the fact that he was an honor student and a member of several academic and social clubs at his school. As we have pointed out earlier in this text, especially in Chapter 6, belonging to and participating in school activities can be a hedge on dropping out of school. Kenneth continues on regarding how he as a migrant student was seen by teachers: "You had some (teachers) who viewed us as not being capable of learning like the ones who just stayed in one area, who had decent jobs, whose parents had decent jobs. And you had some (teachers) who recognized us as being just as capable." "In Alabama I had teachers who put us down because we were the only migrants at that high school. We were the only migrant family there, and they had a tendency to put us down, but as far as New York, it was more positive in New York than in Alabama. I guess it's because it's where migrants work heavily, you know." This illustrates that the familiar is accepted, the unfamiliar questioned. Sociologically, the importance of the acceptance of the familiar and the labeling of the unfamiliar as deviant is evident throughout the literature. Kenneth says the students "just viewed us as being students, being somebody, we were a person, you know, and a lot of them viewed us as being just as capable as they were." He goes on to relate, as other students have, that oftentimes teachers took their cues from students on how to interact with these students.

This teacher-cuing behavior is one of the most striking findings of our study and certainly warrants further research. It is a serendipitous find and certainly a valuable one.

Kenneth mentioned earlier that his support for education came from his family. While on The University of Tennessee campus, Kenneth says his support came from the College Assistance Migrant Program (CAMP) and the accounting department. In regards to the CAMP staff, he says, "Although they viewed it as their job to help me, I remember a number of occasions that they went out of their way to help me. And having people like that behind you, it just gives you that extra motive to, you know, hey, you can do it, go for it." These comments illustrate how special programs can aid at-risk students in successfully completing school, even college, and the strong role that self-concept plays in academic achievement. Even though Kenneth is not an at-risk student, he still reports the relevance and importance of this special program.

As far as reality checks and locus of control, Kenneth says, "I view this as being my only chance, because I know my parents cannot afford to send me to college." He sees the opportunity and does not plan on letting it slip away.

When asked if he knew anyone personally who quit school, Kenneth said no. His immediate friends and peers are a related family whose values toward school are the same that he received from his mother and father. When asked if he knew of any dropouts, he said yes and he felt that they left school because, "School for them had no value." Kenneth does not see how school didn't have value for them because for him it did. As mentioned earlier, Kenneth was not only an honor student but also a member of several school clubs and activities. In terms of perceptions or stereotypes of migrants, Kenneth feels that as a migrant he did not stand out in any way.

If anything, one learns from this chapter as well as this interview that one must be very careful in stereotyping any group and certainly, in this case, migrants.

Chapter 12

MIGRANT AND SEASONAL FARMWORKERS AND DROPPING OUT

Loida C. Velázquez

"Always on the way. Always goin'. Seems to me we don't never come to nothin." This quote from John Steinbeck's novel *Grapes of Wrath* is still appropriately used to describe the plight of the migrant farmworker all over the world. In the United States. migrant farmworkers have been labeled the most disadvantaged of all minority groups. An invisible group to most of society, they are, by definition, families on the move with little time to establish community ties (Ford, 1988). They live in isolation even when working in high-density areas. When they stop to work in local farms, they are hardly noticed by most community members (Prewitt-Diaz, Trotter, & Rivera, 1990). For the most part their needs, problems, dreams, and aspirations are kept hidden and go unmet and unfulfilled.

Migrant workers are defined as those persons who are agricultural laborers and who travel within the geographical boundaries of the continental United States and Canada in pursuit of employment. These migrant workers move along three identifiable streams: the eastern stream, the Mid-Continent stream, and the West Coast stream (King-Stoops, 1980). The eastern stream is made up of Puerto Ricans, Mexican-Americans, Anglos, Canadian Indians, and Blacks, and flows mostly up and down the region east of the Appalachian mountains. The Mid-Continent stream, composed of Mexicans, Mexican-Americans, Blacks, and most recently Vietnamese and Cambodians, traces the Mississippi river basin; Mid-Continent stream migrants move to and from different regions in Texas. The West Coast stream is the largest movement, extending from California and Arizona to Oregon and Washington. This stream is composed primarily of documented and undocumented Mexicans, Central Americans,

Vietnamese, Filipinos, and other western Pacific immigrants.

Migrants are the most undereducated major sub-group in the United States. According to the National Council of La Raza (1990), their high school dropout rate (43%) is larger than any other group. Mobility, language, and cultural differences experienced as they move from one community to another combine with health and nutritional problems to have a negative effect on school achievement. The constant interruption of migrants' educational process, as well as the inability of schools to understand their culture and meet their needs, leads to confusion, frustration, and a feeling of alienation among migrants. This feeling of alienation becomes a major factor in the incidence of migrant students dropping out of school. Hodgkinson (1985) reports that over 70 percent of all migrants have not completed high school and 75 percent are functionally illiterate.

The Culture of Migrancy: Values and Beliefs

A culture is defined as the set of distinctive modes or ways of behaving that are shared by a group. Migrant lifestyles revolve around working, moving on to find other work, and working again. The activities involved in this process have created behavioral patterns that some researchers (Prewitt-Diaz, Trotter, & Rivera, 1990), have called "the culture of migrancy." These behavioral patterns were observed throughout the three streams and reported independently by ethnographers as occurring among people from different ethno-cultural backgrounds (1990, p.117). Hintz studied a community of migrant workers in Ohio and described the migrant culture as follows:

> Migrant workers have a strong sense of family loyalty; respect for elderly persons; politeness; the children do not tease or 'kid' an adult. They have pride for what they are and their heritage; maintain faith with the family and their religion. Migrant workers do not strive to obtain higher salaries and do not want more than they need. They consider their employers, and anglos generally, as "greedy" not satisfied, always wanting more. The migrant family stands firm in its values. They feel that diplomacy and tactfulness are very important in communicating with others. They are not demanding or aggressive towards agencies or employers. They are not likely to exert violent actions politically. (1981, p. 13)

The ethnographic study by Prewitt-Diaz and others focused on migrant children and in the process increased our understanding of migrant families and their shared behavior patterns. Some of the patterns mentioned in the Prewitt-Diaz study are described in the following paragraphs.

Gender Roles. Although differences are found along ethnic lines, in most cases women are expected to both work in the fields and do household chores. Men and children are usually exempt from household responsibilities.

Marriage at a young age is common for migrants. Marriage signals the end of schooling, especially for female migrants. A few married young men stay in school; women commonly do not. With marriage comes the assumption of adult roles for both sexes. In most migrant families there is enormous pressure for the males to support the family and for females to have children. These complementary roles help young migrant couples survive but severely limit their chances for educational success and advancement.

Adult/Child Roles. Although all cultures differentiate between adult roles and children's behavior, the age at which children begin to adopt adult roles is different for different cultures. In many migrant families, boys begin to be treated as adults when, at age 15 or 16, they can earn as much in the fields as their fathers. Girls start being treated as adults when they are capable of having children and managing a household. The difference between the role expectations of migrant families and those of the dominant society has serious consequences for educational programs. Most migrant children drop out of school when they are able to work in the fields and earn money. Since there is no tradition of mandatory education in their culture of origin, most migrant parents allow their children to make the decision between dropping out of, or staying in, school once they are able to contribute to the family's sustenance.

Dealing with Social Institutions. Educational, health care, and social service agencies are created to facilitate living in a complex society. One of the functions of culture is to teach people how to best use this system of agencies. Migrants, especially those who come from a different linguistic and cultural background, are at a serious disadvantage because they do not understand the system. Some migrants strive to be independent and take pride in meeting their family needs; others suffer in silence because they do not know who could help them in time of trouble.

Powerlessness and the Migrant Cycle. The cycle of migrancy is very hard to break and many migrants feel trapped, with little hope for a better future for their children. This feeling of powerlessness is sometimes misinterpreted as apathy by educational agencies. Although migrant parents express support for their children's education, they also feel that migrancy is their children's fate.

Attitude Toward Authority. Migrants have a generally positive attitude toward authority, especially toward the schools. However, this attitude is occasionally expressed in a way that is culturally confusing to school personnel. For example, migrant parents trust the schools to know what is right for their children and feel that questions about the appropriateness of their children's educational program will be construed as a challenge to the teacher's authority and prestige. The institution with which migrants most often interact is the school; paradoxically, the migrant lifestyle is the greatest impediment to their children's educational success.

Migrant's Perceptions of Schooling, Learning, and Education

Perceptions are mental images we form based on our daily experiences. They are the lenses through which we see and interpret the world. A recent ethnographic study of a Hispanic migrant community in Western North Carolina (Velázquez, 1993) focused on migrant adults' perceptions of schooling, learning, and education as a means to better understand their dropout behavior.

The migrant adults interviewed at the ethnographic study site presented a common perception of negative schooling experiences. The constant moving from one place to another and the pressures to conform and to meet expectations proved to be a heavy burden. Nowhere did they indicate that efforts were made by the schools to help these young adults adjust. Many had to repeat grades and were left behind by age peers. Even those who were not turned off by school did not find the right atmosphere to discuss home problems. Others expressed open resentment for the insensitivity of teachers and administrators. All they remembered was the pain, rejection, and isolation. These feelings facilitated the decision to quit school before completing high school requirements.

Schooling as a Painful Experience

Pain is a topic not often discussed in educational circles, yet many of the recent ethnographic studies of dropout students have given voice to experiences painfully engraved in the memories of participants. Quigley (1991a) described those students as "wounded by the schooling system" (p.11). The migrant adults profiled by the ethnographic study revealed strong memories of pain, rejection, and fear. These students felt powerless, personally isolated, and felt they had no control over the events affecting their school life.

The defensive response to school as a painful place is alienation. Seeman (1975) further defined alienation as a feeling of powerlessness, meaninglessness, and personal isolation. For the research study participants' alienation was manifested in two ways: lack of connection with school processes and isolation. Ogbu (1990) blames schools for creating this kind of response in students. According to him, generations of minority students have been discouraged from investing time and efforts in education and have dropped out or emotionally tuned out from what is going on in school.

Another aspect of this theme is school as a source of pressure. Many of the migrants studied talked about the many pressures they had to contend with: growing up poor, being in a family that was constantly moving, having to help with the care of younger siblings, and having to supplement the household income with outside work. School was therefore seen as an extra pressure.

Gibson (1993) compared the pressures migrant students endure with other minority students and noted that they also view schooling with suspicion and ambivalence because it pressures them to conform to the dominant culture and to reject the values and beliefs of their culture. The student concludes that the acquisition of skills in the dominant culture, together with the acceptance of teacher authority and school rules, are challenges that need to be resisted.

School as a Meaningless Place

The view of school as a meaningless place is described often in the dropout research literature (Bishop, 1989; McLeod, 1987; Fordham & Ogbu, 1986). Some of these studies define meaninglessness as the connection or lack of connection between schools and orientation toward the future; specifically a lack of orientation toward finding a job. For migrants and their children, the relationship between schooling and their future is even less clear than for families with a more stable source of income. Many migrants' families feel there is nothing else they can do but farm work. For the majority of the people interviewed, migrancy had become a family tradition. Some were the fourth generation of a family whose main source of income was migrant farm work. They felt trapped into doing farmwork because when they tried to do something else they were not paid as well.

Since the laws controlling child labor allow thirteen-years-olds to do farm work, a migrant family whose subsistence depends on seasonal work will view it as better for the whole family if the children are able to increase the family income by joining them in the fields. Children can make a significant contribution to the household income, one that can make the difference between survival and despair. Schooling is not viewed as a means to find better employment.

The migrant adults in the Velázquez (1993) study left school for a variety of reasons. Some of those reasons were the same expressed by members of other ethnic groups, but some were unique to the migrant lifestyle. Families that migrate in order to find work become part of a complex lifestyle that affects the entire family. The decision to migrate is essentially a financial one, but its consequences include negatives effects on social relationships, health, and educational opportunities. School officials concerned about the high rate of dropout behavior among Hispanics consider migrant labor a deterrent to education, since it provides access to money at an early age.

Ogbu (1990) found that minority students resist the school culture by practicing a system of cultural inversion; that is, by exhibiting behaviors that are contrary to the expectations of school administrators. He stated that minorities in the United States have historically been excluded from the high-quality education received by white students and consistently been denied access to viable jobs. In her study on urban adolescents, Fine (1986) concluded: "Whether dropping out is a personal act of rejection, assertion, joining one's peers, or giving up, it presumes a structural context that is being rejected, critiqued, and/or experienced as defeating by the actor" (p. 397).

Dropping Out as an Accepted Solution to a Difficult Situation

Among migrants, dropping out from school is as much a family pattern as migrant work. Most of the study participants had parents and/or siblings who were also migrant workers and who had dropped out of school at an early age. Of the migrant students enrolled in a

High School Equivalency Program between 1987 and 1990, 78 percent dropped out of school between the seventh and ninth grades. Cranston, Platt, and Martinez (1993) studied the self-esteem of migrant youth and found that the research participants showed decreased self-esteem as grade level increased, reaching the lowest point at grade eight. Most of the students in the Velázquez study also left school before entering high school or around eighth grade.

In a survey by Apicella (1985), migrant dropout students gave the following reasons for leaving school: failing classes; did not like school; had very few credits for graduation; had to work; family needed money; did not feel a part of school; had problems with teacher; felt older than other students; got suspended and did not go back; and had problems with other students.

Both Apicella (1985) and Velázquez (1993) found that migrant students were dissatisfied with their early school experiences. Yet, they consistently expressed a belief in the value of education, especially for their children. They expressed pride in learning on their own, during and after leaving schooling. Since, however, their own schooling experience resulted in alienation, dissatisfaction, and resentment, the result was distrust in schooling as a means for improving employability and quality of life.

Dropping Out as Not Synonymous with Rejection of Learning

Adult education research examining non-participation in adult basic education programs has traditionally focused either on school dropouts' psychosocial deficiencies or on barriers or deterrents to participation (Boshier, 1973; Hayes, 1989; Valentine & Darkenwald, 1990). However, in recent years resistance theory has changed the research focus to the issue of schooling and its impact on students.

Based on Marx's (1969) statement that "every social process of production is at the same time a process of reproduction" (p. 531), radical educators have looked at school as an institution whose main function is the reproduction of the dominant ideology. Instead of blaming students for academic failure or non-participation, they blame the dominant society. According to Giroux (1983), recent research in schooling has attempted to move beyond reproduction theories. This research emphasizes the importance of human volition, struggle, and resistance to reproduction. Resistance theorists have attempted to demonstrate that the mechanism of social and cultural reproduction is never complete and always meets with partially realized elements of opposition. Quigley (1990, 1991, 1992) studied school dropouts from the reproduction and resistance perspective. His studies found that these young adults resisted schooling in their earlier years and are now resisting adult basic education programs for the same reasons. He concluded that school resisters were not rejecting learning, but schooling.

Although all of the migrant participants in the Velázquez (1993) ethnographic study were school dropouts, they were active learners. When asked about learning experiences since leaving school, all had a lot to tell. Some talked about street learning, others showed pride in learning skills on their own, while others told about their experiences in adult education programs.

Most of the migrant students profiled in the study had tried to continue their education through Adult Basic Education (ABE) programs. It seemed that their initial contact with traditional ABE/GED programs was affected by their negative perceptions of schooling. It was only when they were recruited by a program specially designed for migrant adults that they were able to overcome these perceptions and view education as a means to better employment and personal satisfaction. All but one completed high school requirements once they found the appropriate program.

All the migrant adults profiled provided vivid and glowing comments about their belief in the value of education for themselves and their children. Despite the fact that their parents had little schooling and they themselves had not completed high school, most parents wanted their children to finish school. Resistance theory suggests that some school dropout students operate from a different set of values than does the school system. Some researchers have concluded that these students value "doing" over mental activity and leave school when schooling no longer meet those values. Consequently, they might experience a greater sense of confidence and self-esteem after leaving school (Beder, 1991; Ziegahn, 1992). For many, "learning can be embraced only after it has been mentally disassociated from formal education memories" (Ziegahn, 1992, p. 34).

An Example of a Successful Learning Experience for Migrants

The University of Tennessee High School Equivalency Program (HEP) , a project funded by the U.S. Department of Education, has been praised by many because of its uniqueness. Funded to serve exclusively migrant and seasonal farmworkers who drop out of school, it was designed to meet their particular needs. There are 20 other HEP projects through the nation but most are residential programs housed by institutions of higher education. The University of Tennessee HEP is a multiple site project that was designed following principles of community-based programs. The program's schedule is flexible, giving students the opportunity to attend at their own convenience. It is staffed by bilingual teachers (English and Spanish) who are experienced working with the migrant population. It provides transportation and a stipend for incidental expenses. It is not curriculum-driven but student-centered. Its goal is to empower students through education and to assist them to become integrated into the local community.

The UT-HEP project has been nationally recognized as a good example of a program for migrant dropouts. A quick evaluation of the factors contributing to the overall success of this program in reaching migrants reveals characteristics of effective dropout retrieval programs:

1. The program is geared to empower students by increasing success experiences, self-confidence, and feelings of self-worth and dignity.

2. Placement plans start at enrollment and placement activities are geared to end in post-secondary education or competitive employment.

3. Class schedule is flexible with a choice of morning, afternoon, or evening classes. Students unable to attend classes are allowed to take home the instructional material. The instructors and counselors will periodically check with the student either by phone or a home visit.

4. A strong promotion and recruitment program is maintained through visits to migrant gathering places such as laundromats, the migrant clinic, the Mexican store, the Spanish-speaking church, and the migrant housing section of town.

5. Coordinators, recruiters, counselors, and instructors are culturally and ethnically representative of the student body.

6. Bilingual counselors are available and an intensive personal and career counseling program is implemented.

7. An individually tailored educational and placement plan is developed with the student leading the activity.

8. Staff receive regular training in adult education and culturally sensitive topics.

9. Teacher and program effectiveness are regularly evaluated. The evaluation is staff initiated and has student contribution.

Conclusion

Federal legislation in the United States concerning migrant and seasonal farmworkers has historically included regulatory measures designed to improve substandard working, occupational health, housing, and educational conditions encountered by this segment of the population. In 1964, as part of an overall strategy in educational issues, program priority was given to the children of migrant and seasonal farmworkers. Federal funding became available for programs that intended to document, coordinate, and supplement their education. The paradigm shift in federal support that began in the early 1990s completely disbanded many of those programs. Programs for special populations are no longer popular and a philosophy of "one size fits all" has taken over. The High School Equivalency Program and it's sister program, the College Assistance Migrant Program were also targeted for extinction by the 1997 presidential budget and remained alive for another year after a last minute infusion of funds into the budget for the Federal Department of Education. These programs are not expected to survive beyond 1998.

Despite funding decisions, research continues to show that the early experiences of migrant youth related to schooling, learning, and education have made a silent, unconscious impact in their lives. These experiences have helped shape their frame of reference and continue to condition their attitudes and behaviors. The migrant community is the context where these experiences were interpreted. Dropout retrieval programs trying to reach migrants need to examine the basic perceptions from which their attitudes and behaviors flow and the cultural context that gives meaning to these perceptions. Ethnographic studies seem to be the most appropriate way of unraveling the multiple aspects influencing migrant students educational decisions. Quigley (1992) stated it this way: "The decision to participate in literacy needs to be seen through the kaleidoscope of sociological influences, not the least of which is the impact of past schooling" (p.211).

Community-based education seems to be the appropriate vehicle for addressing the needs of a culturally diverse population, especially migrant farm workers. The following recommendations are made based on the belief that a successful dropout retrieval program depends in great extent on how it responds to the cultural, political, socioeconomic, and experiential realities of the participants:

- Research the target community and learn about its culture and its members past schooling experiences.
- Design the project around the goal of assisting participants to integrate into the local community. Assist the local community in learning about and receiving migrant farmworkers into their midst.
- Provide an open and supportive environment and assist migrant farmworkers to overcome negative memories of schooling.
- Build a strong network of community resources.
- Offer classes that are flexible; involve migrant students in the process of designing their own learning experiences.
- Carefully select teachers and tutors that can serve as facilitators and are knowledgeable of participants' cultural norms.
- Adopt instructional strategies based in group dialogue, personal interaction, and active participation. Design a curriculum that integrates basic skills with personal and community development activities.

Chapter 13

NONCURRICULAR CHANGES

If one thing jumps out at us in our study of dropouts, pushouts, and at-risk children, it is that so much has happened to them at such an early age. Their family lives have been touched by alcoholism, drug abuse, physical, sexual, and mental abuse, and some of our subjects have even been present when their fathers were murdered. There is no question that there are significant differences between persisters and dropouts, and the differences run far beyond their respective performances in school.

At the alternative school described in Chapter 9, 17 of 21 girls have signed up to be in a group for those who have been raped. More has been perpetrated upon these young people than can be imagined, and it is our opinion that it is amazing that they didn't manifest school problems earlier or quit entirely earlier in their school career. Given the multiplicity and severity of their problems, it is a sure bet that these young people are, or will be soon, candidates for human service care.

The term human services as used in this text is of a special philosophy and sees persons as not having one problem but as being beset with multiple problems. The human service philosophy is uniquely suited to the needs of at-risk, dropout, and pushout students. The model of human services has the following five steps (Kronick, 1982, p. 3):

1. The academic approach is multidisciplinary.
2. The social welfare system should be coordinated.
3. A problem-solving approach is to be followed.
4. A generalist model is the one to be used.
5. There should be a concern for the total person.

The Human Service Model as proposed here is of special relevance to our target population because it is beset by so many problems beyond the range of the school. The question is often asked, "Which comes first? Poor performance in the classroom or learning disabilities or emotional disturbance." It is our philosophy that working on the two problem areas simultaneously is the most propitious way in which to cut down on emotional problems and increase appropriate classroom behavior.

A definition of human services is given by Mehr (1986):

> Human services is the field of endeavor that helps individuals cope with problems in living which are expressed in psychological, behavioral, or legal terminology and that is characterized by an integrated pragmatic approach focusing on problem solution within the client's life space utilizing change strategies affecting both the internal person and his or her external environment. (p. 19.)

The focus on problems in living is appropriate for dropout-prone students because they do have so many problems in living, beyond what they face in school. The human service focus on the total person reflects a concern for more than the school problems. The multidisciplinary approach reflects an understanding that knowledge of human behavior comes from more than one academic area and that interventions based on this knowledge are more theoretically sound if they come from a multidisciplinary base. It is assumed that these interventions will be applied more effectively if the helper is aware of a multidisciplinary approach to helping.

A coordinated social welfare system is the desired state for both helper and student, but more often than not, this is an ideal rather than actual state. The at-risk student is often seen by corrections, mental health, or welfare workers, along with school counselors. It is often the case that these human service providers are not aware of what the other is doing. It would also make for a much stronger case if there was interagency as well as intraagency coordination in working with this group of students who are at risk. Implied in all this is that the human service worker helps the total person and so, with his/her multidisciplinary background, must coordinate the efforts of all involved. A concern for the total person reflects that the student's dropout behavior is affected by many variables that need attention.

If we were to look at this situation in a modular fashion, dropout behavior could be seen as an intervening variable between intelligence, race, gender, reading ability, being retained a grade, participation in school activities, involvement in crime, being on welfare, and/or being treated for emotional problems. These variables are so dynamic that a very sophisticated model would have to be designed to determine time order, but it is our assumption that the time order presented here is logical. Figure 3 is an illustration of how this process might be viewed.

Figure 3

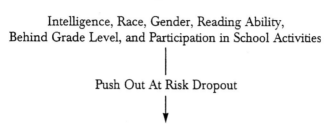

Intelligence, Race, Gender, Reading Ability,
Behind Grade Level, and Participation in School Activities

Push Out At Risk Dropout

Involvement in Crime, Treatment for Mental Illness, and on Welfare

From all of this, the human service worker takes a generalist approach to working with dropouts, realizing that the dropout has many problems, not one, and that a concern for the needs of the total person requires a generalist approach to practice. Mandell and Schram (1985, pp. 17–18) list nine barriers that exist in delivery of human services. These barriers are most appropriate for at-risk children.

1. **The difficulty of knowing how serious the problem is.** The problem of definition of dropouts leads to the problem of not knowing how many dropout students there are. School districts that are defensive hold the dropout figures down, while the districts that might want grant funds push the figures up. In most instances, because of the problems of definition and data gathering, the school districts don't know what the dropout rate is.
2. **The need to deny the gravity of the problem.** As stated above, the school system may not want to report the dropout level for fear that it reflects negatively on the system. This may lead to shakeups within the system and realignment of job positions.
3. **The fear of being judged, labeled, or punished.** School systems, being the political animals they are, especially when the superintendent is elected, certainly do not want to be labeled as failures in the schooling of our children.
4. **The suspicion or distrust of human service workers and agencies.** Given the fact that so many of the families have had experiences with human service agencies, not all of which have been favorable, it is certainly no surprise that they may be reluctant to come

forward for help for their child who is not doing well or simply not going to school. Items 1, 2, and 3 could also be used to describe why the client rather than the school is reluctant to come for help. Obviously, the three factors might keep families with dropout-prone children from seeking help.

5. **The shame of not being able to solve one's own problems.** This can also be attributed to the school system or the family. In fact, this dichotomy of school and family may be artificial in trying to describe the problems of at-risk children where the child's problems in living are ecological.

6. **Fear of the unknown, of change, and of unpredictability.** Those of us who have been in human service work for any period of time know that too often the system is where the intervention is needed, but too seldom is this where it is actually done. The story of the man/woman looking for his keys under the streetlight where it was easier rather than in the dark where he/she lost them is illustrative of the problem of system change. Throughout this text, we have seen that the school system is resistant to change.

7. **The inadequacy of services.** Many students and families have had an unfavorable experience with a human service agency and believe that this will generalize to future situations. Primers on how to be good consumers would be useful for clients who find the human service system mystifying. Human services may be inadequate due to lack of funding or may appear inadequate to the client because of his or her lack of experience with the system.

8. **The difficulties of choosing the appropriate program and helper.** As mentioned above, the human service system is mystifying to many people, and choosing the appropriate program or helper is most difficult. The problem of whether the child has a learning disability or is emotionally disturbed is typical of the dilemma of which programs or helpers to choose. Many of these families have been seeing human service providers with their myriad problems for years and see little if any progress being made.

9. **Public image of the program may keep many potential clients from seeking services.** The school may have a negative image, also. Consequently, many parents express no problems with and often support their children in leaving school.

There are an array of human services for at-risk children and their families. The issue is how to get the services to those who need them.

Teamwork

As noted earlier in this chapter, dropout-prone children are often seen by caseworkers from a variety of agencies. A concept that is very important in the delivery of human services, but one that is seldom discussed, is teamwork. Human service providers often work in teams, but there is precious little in their academic preparation that educates them for this process. Brill (1976) defines

> teamwork as that work which is done by a group of people who possess individual expertise, who are responsible for making individual decisions, who hold a common purpose, and who meet together to communicate, share, and consolidate knowledge from which plans are made, future decisions are influenced, and actions are determined. (p. 16.)

This phenomenon of teamwork is one which is most compatible with the philosophy of human services expressed in this chapter and one which fits the needs of at-risk youth about to leave school before graduation. Brill (1976) continues on regarding what a team is. She says,

> a team is a group. As such, the members individually and totally are subject to all of the pressures and forces that operate within a group. The team constitutes a system and partakes of the basic characteristics of systems. It is a whole made up of interrelated parts, existing in a state of dynamic balance. Change in any one part of that system requires concomitant change in the others. In addition to these internal relationships, each team is involved in relationships with the other systems that make up its environment. (p. 22.)

A team approach may also be based on role theory where the team is defined as a system of interlocking roles, where roles are seen as the sum total of the behaviors expected from a person who occupies a particular position and status in a social pattern. Roles that may exist include leadership, specialist, and generalist or case manager.

The main problem of teams centers around integration of such a wide variety of practitioners into a democratic team model and development of complementary and supplementary role definitions of them. The team member must find satisfaction in doing for rather than with his/her clients.

It is our contention that greater attention to teamwork is of ultimate importance in human service work, but especially for working with dropouts. Being that prevention is a possibility in working with dropouts in regards to welfare, crime, or mental illness, the team concept may be of special importance.

Teens Against Crime*

In continually searching for interventions and preventions for the dropout, programs of all sorts are examined and possibly instituted. Teens Against Crime is one such program. Teens Against Crime is operated in cooperation with and funded by The National Crime Prevention Council (1700 K Street NW, 2nd Floor, Washington, DC 20006, Phone 202-466-NCPC) and the National Institute for Citizen Education in the Law (Georgetown Law Center, 600 New Jersey Avenue, Washington, DC 20001, Phone 202-662-9620), as a part of their Teens, Crime, and the Community Program. Teens Against Crime is conducted by Access to Action, Inc. with the cooperation of the Knox County Schools, the Knoxville City Police Department, and the Knox County Sheriff's Department. This program is designed to involve teens in an organized way in the community of teens and the community at large. Even though the program is not geared to dropouts and dropout prevention, there are several facets of it that may in fact make it a part of the armature that works in preventing dropouts.

Mediation, crime watch, and peer counseling are three programs that are central to Teens Against Crime. Peer counseling looks at such topics as child abuse. Crime watch is concerned with crime in general and recognizes that teens are disproportionately often crime victims. Mediation is one program that could be used as a dropout prevention mechanism. A mediation board is generally composed of twenty members of which four may serve on any one panel at any one time. Teens are picked who themselves might be in trouble to serve on this panel. Mediation is designed to be an alternate disciplinary route where everyone wins and there are no losers. The roles on the mediation panel might include recorder, observer, assistant mediator, and chief mediator. The chief mediator sets the rules whereby the participants agree to sit during the

---

*I am indebted to Professor Grayfred Gray of The University of Tennessee, Knoxville College of Law for the information on the Teens Against Crime program.

proceedings, be respectful, observe confidentiality, and follow the rules of the mediation board. Four steps are included in the mediation process: (1) statement of the problem; (2) statement of feelings; (3) role reversal; and (4) statement of concrete options.

It is our contention and one that is borne out by our current findings that if children participate in school activities, they are much more likely to stay in school. The Teens Against Crime program, though not designed to keep teens in school, must surely aid in keeping them there.

The Impact of Business

If one wants to take a cynical view regarding problems in education, we could say that dropouts are not seen as a problem until we become aware that they cost us money. This is where the business community comes into focus. When business became aware that dropouts cost them money, the issue became one of social awareness. Dropouts are not good consumers. They do not make enough money to participate fully in America's economy. At the same time, dropouts are underemployed and do not pay the amount of taxes they would if more fully employed. Dropouts are not good employees. It has become acutely evident that the number of dropouts and semi-literate individuals in the work force puts us at an extreme disadvantage when it comes to competing in the world's marketplace. It might be said that competitive labor bills have done more to bring attention to dropouts than any educational imperative. The impetus from business, however, is based on money, not altruism.

Nevertheless, it appears that a strong move will be made by the business community to move into the field of education. Whittle Communications Channel One and Dollywood Incorporated are two examples of business becoming involved in education. Channel One is a controversial news format program that operates under the assumption that high school students do not watch the news. Current knowledge will be tested by assessing the groups that saw Channel One and comparing them with control groups that did not. Whittle gave television monitors, VCRs, and other equipment to those schools selected to be in the pilot program. Commercials that were part of the news segment have added to the controversy and have brought several educational groups, including the National Education Association, out against the Whittle program. However, Chairman Chris Whittle said, "Whittle Communications does not need the support of national education groups to have a successful satellite news program in the country's classrooms. Channel One can work without national support, because education is still locally controlled (*Knoxville News-Sentinel,* 4-21-89, p. C-5).

Dollywood Incorporated, through Dolly Parton, has contributed several thousand dollars to Sevier County, Tennessee to keep students in school. The program has also contributed $500 per student for those students staying in school and attending a regional community college. Dolly Parton has taken a strong interest in seeing that the students of Sevier County, Tennessee finish school. Although a philanthropic undertaking, this allows Dollywood the opportunity to have a better pool from which to select its employees.

The business education nexus is gaining impetus across the country, and Boston is the first place where city-wide support has come together, marshalled by the city's business and educational leaders and structured through an objective-based agreement between the public schools and leading corporations, universities, and trade unions. The Boston Compact combines targeted programs for dropout-prone youth with systematic changes in the way the schools' curricula and instruction are organized. The Compact acknowledges the importance of expanding employment opportunities and access to higher education, and for that purpose it combines the resources of the business, trade, and university communities (Orr, 1987).

The Private Industrial Council (PIC) has been at the heart of many business education ventures. In Boston, the PIC and the Job Collaborative Program strengthened the link between schools and business. The PIC's Summer Jobs program in Boston has been placing youth in private sector summer jobs since 1981. The PIC solicits summer job placements for the students. Companies are asked to pledge jobs or to contribute the salary equivalent for a student to be placed in a private sector job. In 1986 the PIC placed 2,600 students in summer jobs in Boston (Orr, 1987).

The Boston Compact

In September 1982, Boston's public schools and the business community formally launched the Boston Compact. This was a joint pledge to improve the quality of educational preparation and access to employment for Boston's public high school students. According to the terms of the Compact, the Boston public schools agreed to reduce the dropout rate by 5 percent annually and to work toward annual increases in attendance and performance on standardized tests. The schools would improve basic skills training in performance on required minimum competency reading and math tests for all 1986 graduates. The business community's side of the bargain was a promise to give priority in hiring to a specific number of public school graduates, to increase the number of summer jobs for in-school youth, to sign up at least 200 companies for a priority hiring effort, and to expand the PIC's Job Collaborative Program.

The premise of the agreement was that efforts for middle and high school students should be tied to clearly perceivable employment experiences and opportunities. Implied was the belief that poor academic performance of Boston Public School students is a community and business responsibility.

The first signers of the Boston Compact were a group of twenty-five executive officers from the city's largest companies who were concerned about the problems of Boston's public schools. Since the late 1950s, these leaders had worked cooperatively as a coordinating council known informally as The Vault on areas of social responsibility. Their prominence in the business community drew others to join the compact. The only strong complaint was from the black community which requested and received assurances that minority youth would be employed in percentages reflective of their proportion in the school system. With this addition, the Boston Compact was officially signed on September 22, 1982. (Orr, 1987, p. 180)

The Boston Compact reflects that business and education can work together, but that commitment from the top is critical if the program is to succeed. By having the involvement of the chief executive officers of the major corporations involved, the possibilities of success are enhanced. Even with this impressive-looking program in place, the dropout rate was not affected. The high dropout rates persisted. In order to combat this, another program, Compact Ventures, was developed. This program targeted high-risk ninth graders and was designed to improve academic achievement through supportive services, reorganization of the ninth grade into clusters, and employment opportunity incentives.

The Boston PIC did a process evaluation and is making changes based on what was found. The preliminary outcome evaluation showed that the dropout rate had not been reduced. Nonetheless, this is a model program because of its evaluation components and adjustments that are being made from what is learned from these evaluations.

B.E.S.T. Program

Knoxville business becomes involved in education because it wants to upgrade the quality of its employee pool. One business leader and former school board member says, "Most businessmen have never given it really careful thought" (the education of future workers). However, he says of a business elite, "He said to me, 'We've got to do something for these kids to help them out, train them to get a job.'"

The involvement of these community elites, according to our respondent, makes credibility instant. One example of business' involvement in education that is most positive is BUSINESS ENCOURAGES STUDENTS AND TEACHERS "B.E.S.T." B.E.S.T. gave $1,000 awards to schools, principals, and teachers. In 1989 alone, at least $30,000 was given by the B.E.S.T. program to education in one local community. (The B.E.S.T. program is funded through the Knoxville, Tennessee Chamber of Commerce.)

Programs like B.E.S.T. and the Boston Compact show that there is a possibility that education and business can work together in a positive and constructive manner. The data on workers of the future show that it is no longer a luxury but a must that education and business work together in educating public school students in the 1990s.

Chapter 14

SOME CURRENT PREVENTION PRACTICES

The dropout is someone who is likely to end up in corrections, mental health, or on welfare upon reaching adulthood. But whether the out-of-school student is involved in delinquent behavior while he or she is not in school is not so clear. Thornberry, Moore, and Christenson (1985), in their study of dropouts' involvement in criminal behavior, explore the merits of both Control and Strain Theory, which we have discussed in Chapter 7. They point out that most studies have not taken into consideration time lapse in evaluating the explanatory power of Strain and Control Theory.

In *Strain Theory* (Cohen, 1955; Cloward & Ohlin, 1960), the middle-class environment of the school is viewed as a major source of frustration and alienation for lower-class youth. To alleviate their frustration, these students withdraw legitimacy from middle-class norms and turn to delinquency as a source of success, status, and approval. Thus, for lower-class students Strain Theory views school and its attendant failure as a major cause of criminal activity. On the other hand, in his formulation of Social Control Theory, Hirschi (1969) posits that delinquency arises when the person's bond to conventional society is weakened. Individuals who are attached to conventional others and committed to conventional institutions are strongly bonded to society and hence are unlikely candidates for crime. Since school is "an imminently conventional institution" (Hirschi, 1969), Social Control Theory views it as a major source of bonding which should reduce delinquent activity.

Strain and Control Theories therefore offer divergent assessments of the relationship between school and delinquency, especially for lower-class youths. In the former, school is a source of failure and frustration which increases delinquent conduct; in the latter, it is a source of social control which decreases delinquent conduct.

Based on these divergent viewpoints, Strain and Control Theory present contradictory predictions concerning the effect of dropping out of high school on subsequent criminal involvement. According to Strain

Theory, because dropping out eliminates the source of frustration brought about by failure in the school, criminal conduct should decline sharply following dropout. According to Control Theory, however, dropping out reduces institutional control; therefore, criminal behavior should increase.

Thornberry, Moore, and Christenson (1985) find more support for Control than Strain Theory when using longer terms for follow-up of involvement in crime. This finding is supported by the common wisdom that dropouts tend to have a greater involvement in crime than persisters, but it does not answer the question as to whether the truant is engaging in delinquent behavior while he or she is truant. It is our assertion that dropping out is strongly correlated with criminal behavior but not necessarily with delinquent behavior. It is our assumption, however, that those juveniles who could be classified as hard-core predatory criminals are not in school, but that they are a very different population of young people than the early school leaver or truant.

An interesting artifact of juvenile court procedure that may occur is that the truant may be put on probation for his or her truancy, and if this probation is violated, the truant may be placed on delinquent status. The conundrum here is that the school wants the court to be the bad guy in this scenario and the court often resists this role. What appears to emerge is that both the court and the school would just as soon see the truant not in school. This may be the appropriate assessment if Strain Theory is correct. It would be counterproductive if Control Theory is correct. Our response to this dilemma would be referral to alternative schools where personal education based on curriculum-based assessment would be followed. A description of an alternative school model is presented in Chapter 8. What we may want to consider here is type of offense and age. Control Theory may be more effective when dealing with younger students and less serious offenders, whereas Strain Theory may be more useful when dealing with older students and more serious offenses.

From initial interviews with at-risk students, it appears that school non-attenders do not tend to be involved in delinquency while they are not in school. Initial findings show that while they are not in school, they tend to be at home watching television. Thus, the main delinquency they are engaging in is the status offense of truancy. Interviews with juvenile court officials, however, reflect that court personnel believe the truant child to be breaking the law while they are not in school. Thus, because of the operation of the juvenile court and its concomitant work with the school system, we should take a close look at which has more effective explanatory power: that of Strain or Control Theory. It appears that certain procedures might even have to be reversed if one theoretical model tends to have stronger explanatory power than another.

The correlation of early school leaving and mental illness tends to be minimal. Our initial hypothesis was that there might be a lot of emotional disturbance among this dropout population, but initial data do not reflect that these young people are being referred for mental health care. Entries into Tennessee state psychiatric hospitals tend to reflect few school-related problems and, for the past two years, to show strong delinquent and criminal justice ties. This is due to an artifact of a juvenile law which says that if a judge refers a student to a facility, that facility must accept that child whether the facility is equipped to handle that particular child's problem or not. A child may be admitted into a psychiatric hospital under one of the following categories: voluntary, involuntary, juvenile court committal order, civil court commitment, transfer from a correctional facility, or emergency. What we find is that the school system now will be dealing with many problem behaviors of children that historically may have been handled by the Department of Corrections or the Department of Mental Health. Thus, as asserted elsewhere, we are throwing more onto the school, asking more of them. As mentioned earlier, it is no longer a question as to whether or not the school will be a parent, it is whether or not the school will be a good parent.

The following five strategies are recommended as steps in defining and intervening with at-risk youth who may be early school leavers.

STEP 1: *Target dropouts early*

There are identifiable classes of behavior which are predictive of dropping out. By targeting students who exhibit these behaviors, intervention strategies designed to deal specifically with those antecedent behaviors can be tested for effectiveness. The identifiable classes of behavior are:

1. Truancy and excessive absences.
2. Little participation in school activities.
3. Low or failing grades in at least two courses.
4. Difficulty communicating with teachers and other students.
5. Exhibiting little interest in classroom work.

STEP 2: Start support programs

Successful students would be used as peer counselors to work with those individuals having trouble in school. Skills that should be emphasized in these peer support groups would include:

a. Social skills.

Targeted students come from environments that do not provide the basic social skills the schools require. These students lack the most rudimentary conversational skills such as saying "yes, no, and thank you." Non-verbal skills, such as maintaining eye contact and using appropriate body language, are examples of the skills which would be taught and reinforced by student peer counselors. Many at-risk students are passive; this passiveness may deteriorate, however, into passive-aggressiveness. These students need to be taught appropriate ways of asserting themselves.

b. Survival skills.

Targeted students need to be taught how to get along in social situations, how to maintain their own sense of identity without resorting to inappropriate physical means, and how to make decisions. They need to learn to evaluate the consequences of the decisions they make. Many of them need to learn to manage their own time. Free time is something many of them lack. In a significant number of instances, potential dropouts are working at outside jobs. A recent newspaper article pointed out that almost 55 percent of Tennessee's high school students work between 20 and 30 hours a week at a job outside school. It is difficult for students who lack time-management skills to stay awake in the classroom when they have worked until midnight the previous night.

c. Study skills.

All students need study skills, but the potential dropout has the greatest need.

STEP 3: Develop interesting extracurricular activities

As mentioned above, potential dropouts are social isolates. They tend to have no stake in school participation and shun involvement in typical school activities. Urging them to get involved in extracurricular activities, and guiding them in the process, would be one way to thwart the development of one of the behaviors correlated with dropping out (see Step 1).

STEP 4: *Establish work-study programs*

These students need to be taught how to move from the academic classroom to the real world; they need to understand the importance of acquiring appropriate job skills.

STEP 5: *Conduct exit interviews*

If a student persists in dropping out, it would be crucial to know why such a choice was made even though all intervention strategies had been tried. It would be useful and informative to conduct a follow-up interview with the student six weeks after dropping out to determine whether there is regret over the decision and whether there are ways to bring him or her back into the school system.

These strategies are capable of being employed by school systems and may be evaluated empirically. Parts of these five steps have been used in past dropout intervention programs. In programs that have been established in Appalachia, for example, interventions have included tutorials, alternative curricula or classes, work-related activities, counseling/ advising sessions, parental involvement strategies, attitudinal self-awareness activities, and attendance incentive schemes. However, no effort appears to have been made to "match" these intervention strategies to particular student behavior profiles. The suggestion proposed here is designed to test the hypothesis that potential dropouts exhibit symptoms that can be matched to specific intervention strategies to reduce the dropout rate of students in grades 7–12.

The five sections discussed here reflect three important ideas. One is the importance of process. The dropout needs to be examined as early as the preschool and first grade years. As some of the data reflect, students begin to plan to drop out as early as the first grade. Dropout prevention, therefore, should be viewed as a linear process spanning kindergarten through the twelfth grade. Second is the idea of involvement. If you can get these students involved in activities occurring in the school setting, they have a vested interest in school. They are then less likely to leave school. Third, a positive self-concept or identity comes with success in the school setting. This is a self-reinforcing phenomenon; that is, school success helps create a positive identity.

One of the more interesting findings from earlier research is that a student's intention to stay in or leave school was determined more by personal attitudes than by how he/she felt others perceived the decision.

This was especially true for males. Females tended to be more influenced than males by how they think others will view their decision to drop out (Orr, 1987).

Programs that emphasize interaction with at-risk students at both micro and macro levels are described by M. T. Orr (1987) in her book, *Keeping Students in School.* The programs she describes range from a peer tutoring program to city-wide approaches that look beyond the school system. The following is a highlight of what she presents describing various programs across the country. The interested reader is of course referred to her text for more in-depth description of these programs. We merely choose to highlight certain programs to give our reader a flavor of what is being done across the country by certain locales to reach at-risk youth.

At the micro level of intervention, Orr (1987) describes the Twelve Together program in Detroit, the Adopt-A–Student program in Atlanta, and the Summer Youth Employment Program in New Bedford, Massachusetts. The Twelve Together program targets ninth graders and focuses on the use of peer counseling to deal with poor self-image, laziness, and alcohol and drug problems. Study time is an hour and a half per day. The Adopt-A–Student program uses business volunteers as mentors for the students. The Summer Youth Employment Program utilizes the services of the Private Industrial Council and the Chamber of Commerce. The children served are JTPA eligible. Interestingly enough, in this project, the Chamber of Commerce generated more jobs than the program could fill. These three programs Orr (1987) labeled as supplemental services. She defines a supplemental services program as "one in which supportive counseling and job readiness preparation are provided to marginally performing students who are still in school." While these programs are limited in scope, they can be enough to encourage some dropout-prone students to complete high school. Programs of this type are best for youth who are likely to drop out because they are not involved in school activities, have poor opinions of themselves, or lack post-high school plans. Support groups and part-time employment are inexpensive ways to assist these youth. These programs can easily be sponsored by organizations of the school or integrated within an existing educational program.

Moving along the continuum from micro- to macro-level programs, Orr (1987) describes programs to remove barriers to continued education. These programs include the Secondary Credit Exchange program, a mutual exchange program between the states of Washington and Texas; the Murray Wright High School Daycare Center in Detroit; and the Adolescent Primary Health Clinic in Houston. The Secondary Credit Exchange Program is of particular interest for several reasons. One is that it makes so much sense that one wonders why there are not more programs like this. Second, the program was started by a second grade teacher on her own initiative with no federal support or grants. Third, the program reaches one of the most difficult dropout-prone groups: the migrant and seasonal worker. The heart of this program is simply that schoolwork, including books and materials, are shipped from Texas to Washington as the child and his or her family follow the crops from Texas to Washington. To graduate, the student must finish the twelfth grade in Texas, however. Because the students are migrants and generally speak English as a second language, there is a need for bilingual teachers. One of the authors, Kronick, is involved in a College Assistance Program to migrants, "CAMP," and a fuller description of migrant children as one group that makes up the at-risk population of young people today is presented in Chapter 9. An incredibly articulate description of this population in the Appalachian and South is given by Robert Coles (1967) and James Agee (1960).

The Murray Wright High School Daycare Center is one of many programs focusing on keeping teenage mothers in school and discouraging future childbearing until after the completion of high school. The program provides education and social services. These types of programs target a part of the at-risk population that leaves school in fairly large numbers. In fact, "pregnancy and starting a family," along with "school was not for me," are by far the most prevalent reasons girls give for leaving school. Model programs of this type are currently in existence in Knoxville and Memphis, Tennessee. The main attack against these types of programs states that they foster and promote promiscuity. The reader is left to his or her own decision on this matter.

The Adolescent Primary Health Care Clinic operates under the assumption that teenage pregnancy and dropping out are correlated, hence the pregnancy issue is a target. Removal of barriers to continued education is designed for youth where economic, family, or personal responsibilities keep them out of school. These programs are structured to help students cope with their competing responsibilities and provide a way for them to complete high school (Orr, 1987).

Comprehensive school-affiliated programs comprise the third set of programs described by Orr (1987). These programs include: the Job Readiness Program in Chicago; Project COFFEE in Oxford, Massachusetts; and Richs Academy in Atlanta.

The Job Readiness Program, along with Project COFFEE and Richs Academy, focus on the relationship between education and future economic security. The focus of these programs is on school attendance and basic skills. There is collaboration with business employers in these programs.

Project COFFEE, along with Richs Academy, focuses on the school business internship. COFFEE requires that student interns be at school before coming to the internship site. The evaluation of Project COFFEE shows it to be successful in regards to attendance, improved basic skills, and a lower dropout rate.

Richs Academy works because of the commitment of top-level management. Initially, it failed because of this lack of commitment. Students who complete the Richs Academy program graduate from Archer High School. The program focuses on self-esteem, attendance, punctuality, and counseling. There appear to be strong similarities between COFFEE and Richs Academy. Current evaluations tend to reveal positive results.

Comprehensive school-affiliated programs are designed for students who are likely to drop out because of serious academic and attendance problems. These programs often combine an array of education, employment, preparation, and counseling services for potential dropouts in a comprehensive multiservice approach that encourages students to remain in school. They are designed to address intensively early manifestations of academic and attendance problems (Orr, 1987).

Services for out-of-school youth comprise the fourth group of programs designed to meet the needs of at-risk youth. Programs included here are Alternative School Networks, and Educational Clinics.

The Educational Clinics described are in Washington State. They are designed to provide short-term educational intervention services to public school dropouts. In addition to instruction and basic academic skills, the clinic provides employment orientation, motivational development, and support services. The clinics are performance-oriented, focusing on academic gains and the courses the student will pursue after leaving the clinic (generally returning to school or completing the GED exam and going on to employment or further education).

The program's philosophy is that individual services can motivate dropouts to change behavior, overcome present problems, and acquire the basic skills that are prerequisite to success in employment and educational endeavors. A medical type of approach (Medical Model) has been adapted using the terms diagnose, prescribe, and treat (Orr, 1987). The Medical Model has a long history within social science but is not the subject of discussion here, other than to raise the question as to whether or not the Medical Model is appropriate and has explanatory power regarding at-risk youth. In contrast to alternative schools, Educational Clinics do not offer academic credit or issue diplomas.

The Alternative School Network described by Orr (1987) is in Chicago. It is a network of 35 community-based alternative schools and youth centers in Chicago and provides a structured program of education, employment preparation, job training, and counseling for youth dropouts throughout inner-city neighborhoods. The network believes in providing young dropouts with an opportunity to learn in a supportive environment while offering services to help modify the causes of truancy and dropping out, and remediating skill deficiencies, all to assist youth in the transition into working life. The instruction is individually designed and self-paced, linking the curriculum to everyday experiences and students' specific needs. Support services offer students counseling and referral to other social services (Orr, 1987).

The present authors are strongly supportive of alternative schools, and a full description of our alternative school model is presented in Chapter 9.

As Orr (1987) moves toward the more macro or systems approach to keeping students in schools, she describes two school system-wide approaches. Discussed here are: The Systematic Approach to Dropout Prevention in New York and the Dropout Prevention and Recovery Program in Los Angeles. The New York program focuses on early signs of dropping out. These include unexcused absences and severe attendance problems in middle-school years. It stresses coordination of resources and placing resources where they are most needed. Because students leave school for so many reasons, this program is comprised of a variety of resources.

The Dropout Prevention and Recovery Program addresses all the levels of schooling equally. This in itself appears to be unique and certainly worthwhile. The project utilizes an outreach consultant to develop parent and community support. At the same time, linkages with businesses to curb dropping out are pursued.

The school system-wide approach acknowledges the school system's responsibility to prevent substantial percentages of students from dropping out. Alternative programs for students at risk of dropping out are combined with consideration of ways to restructure the schools to respond to students' varied educational needs (Orr, 1987).

The final systems-level approach discussed by Orr (1987) is a city-wide approach which she says is looking beyond the school system. The program described is the Boston Compact. The Boston Compact is designed to reduce the number of dropouts, double the number of dropouts enrolled in alternative education programs or schools and to put a dropout prevention task force in place. The Compact reports its greatest success in the improvement of the employment rate of high school graduates. However, the high dropout rates still persist (Orr, 1987).

The city-wide approach draws on the resources of business, universities, and other social agencies. It assumes that dropping out is more than the school system's problem. This approach reflects the idea that the problems that cause students to drop out actually affect a much larger group of students than the dropouts themselves. This realization has stimulated interest in improving the organization of schooling and the incorporating of community services. This philosophy may be tested in the offer from Boston University to take over and run a certain portion of the Boston Public School System.

Much of what Orr (1987) discusses is in concert with our material in Chapter 8. We feel that she has brought and interesting perspective to at-risk students. Her various systems-levels approaches are certainly food for thought when considering interventions aimed at keeping children in school.

Chapter 15

COOPERATION, COORDINATION, AND COLLABORATION – POINTS ALONG A CONTINUUM - FAMILY RESOURCE CENTERS IN RURAL TENNESSEE

ROBERT F. KRONICK AND CAROLYN STINNETT

Introduction

This chapter enters the ongoing debate over coordination of services, cooperation, collaboration and colocation of services regarding the school, family, and community. The high points of this debate appear to be: should the services be provided on school grounds or should the services be physically housed elsewhere? If located on school grounds, the services come with baggage attached to the school, which more often than not is negative. Oftentimes people will not come to the school for help because it is seen as the root of the problem. A second argument against colocation of services is duplication. A third argument for not colocating services with the school is that the cultures of education, human service, and business (a potential player) are so different.

There are powerful reasons for not housing education, translated here as the school, with human services. One is the perceptual set of persons coming for help and their perceptions of service providers. These people may have had bad experiences with the school and human services. They may have only come to the school when summoned because something bad had happened. Too often they are intimidated by the school and are mystified by what goes on there. Schools may do nothing to demystify what is going on; hence, the parents stop coming if they ever came at all. Yet the school may decry the apparent lack of interest by parents, never admitting their role in this process.

Professional conflicts are less forgivable but may be more entrenched. This is a more complicated issue, yet it is an issue that must be addressed. Crowson and Boyd (1996) list four central points that must be addressed when attempting to implement collaborative services. They are: (a) goal structures, (b) institutional interests, (c) environmental controls, and (d) institutional conventions. Goal structures are characterized by a sense of a shared central problem. Institutional interests revolve around the notion of reward structures. Environmental control illustrates how one of the collaborators may co-opt the others. Institutional conventions are housed in what Bolman and Deal (1991) call a symbolic frame. These conventions concern themselves with rituals, stories, and ceremonies (Crowson & Boyd, 1996).

Coordination of services at a colocated site have both internal and external difficulties. The internal difficulties exist because of the lack of understanding of teamwork and the opportunity to practice. Collaborative skills need to be taught and practiced. Realization that collaboration in education and human services is a must within the academy and the world of work.

From the client's perspective, there are several reasons why they will not come for services; and those reasons may mitigate against having human services located within a school. These range from denying the gravity of the problem to a lack of trust of the human service provider (Kronick & Hargis, 1990). Even though this may be sufficient reason to not locate human services within a school, the focus of this chapter is to combine human services and education and to make the school a place where parents and community will feel comfortable when they come for services. The time is now to make schools and human services work together!

It is evident that not all human service problems should be treated with one method, such as teamwork; but the argument of this chapter is that for at-risk students, collaboration is a must.

It appears to be a given that decrimental budgeting is the norm for the rest of the twentieth century. This fact also begs for collaboration in human services.

Definition of Terms

> Essential education, health and human services are often inaccessible or provided in ways that diminish rather than enhance families' abilities to control their own lives. Separate unsolved problems grow into complicated tangles that affect every family member and put children at risk of failing in school and later in life. In the process everyone loses. (Melaville & Blank, 1993, p. 12)

The above quote makes the point for collaborative services. Too often in human services the right hand may seem to not know what the left hand is doing. Coordination should help with this problem.

One of the criticisms of service coordination is duplication. It appears that service coordination may actually lessen service duplication. It will take long-term outcome evaluations to determine whether coordination and colocation of services adds to or lessens duplication of services.

A colloborative is a group who has agreed to be partners in addressing school problems. Collaboration involves people from any areas who share power and work together to accomplish a goal. Collaboration requires partners to put aside their own agendas in favor of common goals. Collaboration is a mind-set that says, of course, I am going to need the help of others to do my job (Melaville & Blank, 1993).

Collaboration has been defined by Lawson and Anderson (1996) as the sharing of common goals and contains the following steps: (a) communication, (b) clear agreements, (c) vital decision making, (d) monitoring and evaluation, (e) recognition and reward, (f) trust, and (g) leadership.

According to Melaville and Blank (1993), a group will know that it is ready for collaboration when all the partners realize that they have a shared problem that no one can solve alone and when they are ready to look beyond their interest to solve it.

As mentioned earlier, internal conflicts exist within human services and education and must be removed so that effective and efficient services may be delivered to persons in need. Earning each others' trust may be the first and most important step in this process.

According to Crowson and Boyd (1996) services may run along a continuum from cooperation to collaboration. Cooperation involves individuals and organizations working together but having their own goals. Collaboration involves various individuals and groups working together and sharing a common set of goals. Seeing the need for coordination and verbalizing the importance of that need is one thing; actually collaborating is something else. Crowson and Boyd (1996) describe five programs that have had varying degrees of success in collaborating, they point out that most programs tend to fall on a line somewhere between cooperation and collaboration with the most common plan being colocation of services.

It appears that organizational cooperation is a very difficult process. It must be done, however, given the financial exigencies that will hover over education and human services for the rest of this century and on into the next. It is ironic that human service workers and teachers are asking clients, groups, and students to do things that they cannot or will not do themselves.

Rural Family Resource Centers in Tennessee

Against the cultural backdrop of Appalachia and East Tennessee, the state has mandated the creation of family resource centers. The ideology of stoicism, individuality, and pride, traits associated with the culture of Appalachia, do not make for an ideal situation for any human service agency, much less one(s) that uses a collaborative approach.

The following quote from Client B is somewhat illustrative of southern and Appalachian culture:

> One of the things that we are really concerned about when we first started putting the program together was that our community has the attitude of you know if it is not broken don't fix it. You know and they don't see anything that is broken. You just put it over in the corner and one day you will get the piece to work. So we were afraid that we would not use the center because it was just like a change. You know why call them? Why do this or why do that? You know my kids are not failing school. But I have been surprised at a lot of the attitudes of the PTA board members and groups like that through the schools that are involved–I really got excited about what Director B is doing and what she is offering. And the community has had a better response like oh what is this? And when I first got involved I thought this program was designed for poverty-level people who are looking for light bills, food, and emergency care; but our middle- and upper-class people have really connected with it too, as far as like oh this is a place where I can go and learn how to do it right! You know, parenting skills and stuff like that. And I am real pleased with that because I thought that most of the people that would respond would be those that would say, "Oh this is another place to get help." But people who don't usually ask for help have said oh! Client B, 1996.

Appalachian culture, according to Best (1986), contains large doses of sensuousness, emotion, and spirituality and promotes inductive reasoning, intuition, creativity, and sensitivity in the arts. These characteristics of culture are not those of K-12 education and put Appalachian students at risk. To further illustrate the counterposition of Appalachian culture with mainstream culture is the cognitive-affective difference between them as seen by the differential use of guilt and shame. "Mountain people, as a rule, are more influenced by shame as a moral force than guilt" (Best, 1986, p 46). The Appalachian people's behavior is far more affective than it is cognitive. "Thought for thought's sake is not a basic product of the culture. The product of thought is usually intimately connected with life as it is being lived by the person doing the thinking" (Best, 1986, p. 46).

The same may be said of language. Rural Appalachian people rarely use more words than are necessary. They are parsimonious with their words; less is better than more. Language is a very important aspect of culture and a colorful one for rural Appalachians. A good example of this is presented in Coles' (1967), classic *Migrants, Sharecroppers and Mountaineers, Volume II, Children in Crisis*: "It is not that she is grim, or glum, or morose, or withdrawn, or stern, or ungiving, or austere, it is that she doesn't need words to give and acknowledge the receipt of messages" (pp. 200-201). In this study, much corroboration was found for the paucity of words for our people. This model holds up for the Coles study and the present one.

The fact that rural Appalachians love their children is borne out also by Coles' (1967) study and in the present study.

"These Appalachian parents certainly do take notice of their children's suffering–for one reason because they are parents and for another because they are traditionally proud and defiant people" (Coles, 1967, p. 264). One of our respondents eloquently illustrates this point by saying:

> I knew that John (son) had a problem because he did not act like any normal child. I first learnt–it first occurred to me when I was at home. I would watch him a lot. See he is adopted. I adopted him and I just wanted to get closer to him and everything. So I spent a lot of time at home with him. I think that helped him a lot and learnt on my own that you could learn a lot from just setting and watching a child, playing with them or spending time with them. I think it helps a lot." Client B, 1996

The parents in our study were excited to learn how to breast-feed, about human development, and other important specifics that would make them better parents.

A final illustration of this point is made by the following:

Most of what we are focusing on is social development and language development. So those are the two big areas. And in talking with parents, I am surprised how many will readily say: "No, he is not where he needs to be." I really expected that there would be a lot of denial, you know with parents saying,
"Oh no, my child is just fine." Anyway, that has really not been the case, so
they have been pretty open and honest about where their child is develop-
mentally.

Another parent had this to say about what she learned at the family resource center regarding her child.

He wasn't behaving well–he was behaving oh, before he came he was
kind of rowdy. Sometimes he didn't want to mind and things like that. And
now they worked with him on that. It has also been easier on me because I did-
n't actually know how to do that–to handle things like that. So they–. He is
learning things, getting ready for kindergarten. So he has learned his ABCs, his
numbers, stuff like that just like you would in kindergarten, so it is getting him
ready for that. And, yeah, if he hadn't come here, he wouldn't really be ready
[for kindergarten]. Client C, 1996

Thaller (1996) says:

Nature provides a tremendous amount of variety in the landscape of
Appalachia. There are tall mountains, fertile valleys and long tenuous lakes.
The four seasons provide endless variety as they slumber in winter gray and
white or blossom in dogwood pink and white or grow green, green and their
blaze with brilliant foliage and tourist brake lights. Appalachia is a region characterized by striking contrast. There are crowded cities and vast expanses of
wilderness. There is a rich supply of natural resources but wide spread poverty. (p. 247)

In a personal vein, Thaller (1996) reminisces:

In my Appalachian family, the main traditional handicraft was the creation of quilts. It was begun as a practical way of recycling the good fabric left
in worn out garments by using the scraps to create warm quilted bed covers.
Out of this it evolved into a hobby and then an art form. My grandmother
loved making quilts. One of my earliest memories is napping under a bright
quilt with butterfly appliques she had pieced and quilted. And although she
passed away many years ago, many of the quilts she made are still bright and
pretty.

But in my family the art form is dying out (of quilt making) since
very few in the younger generation of the family are involved in quilt-
ing. (p. 247)

It is impossible to describe a people or a place in a manner that is
totally truthful but Appalachia has been aptly depicted by Coles

(1967), Verghese (1994), Best (1986), Caudill (1963), Wigginton (1975), and Thaller (1996). To learn more about the people of Appalachia, the interested reader is referred to them.

A Brief History of Family Resource Centers

Given this environment, family resource centers (FRC) were first established in Kentucky. These centers were one way in which the Kentucky educational system responded to the federal mandate to get their schools in order. Other federal guidelines such as the expanding, if you will, of public law 94-142 to include an emphasis on families can also be seen as a precursor to FRCs.

> Within ten years after the start of the first, family resource and support programs, the tone was set for changes in services and systems that continue today. Typically family resource programs exist in community-based programs that may be linked to another organization or stand independently. The FRCs recognize the importance of the fact that a child's sense of self is intrinsically tied to that of his or her parents and that the quality of the parents life is effected by the resources and the environment of the community in which the family lives. The intentional incorporation of family empowerment in all aspects of a program as a way to enhance child development, differentiates FRC programs from other services for families. (Stinnett, 1996, p. 7)

This focus on family and child is based on the social psychological theory of person in context. With emphasis on early child development, the person in context is very important. In this study, all of the FRCs are linked with a school. Hence a great deal of emphasis was placed on the young child or infant and his or her family, regardless of the configuration of the family as single or two-parent, grandparents, or an extended family.

The idea of cooperation, coordination, and collaboration is, of course, an important aspect of the FRCs and the schools. Where on a continuum these programs fell and how effective the programs were is presented in the results section of this chapter.

Three key points play a large part in the philosophy of the FRC focus on families. They are:

1. The definition of family is varied and each family should be approached as a unique system.
2. With few exceptions, people of all ages can best develop by remaining with family or relying on them as an important resource.

3. Families have the potential to change and most troubled families want to do so (Stinnett, 1996).

From the Kentucky plan mentioned earlier in this section came the following four points regarding FRCs:

1. All children can learn and most at high levels too.
2. An atmosphere must be created which empowers the participant or consumer to acquire the confidence necessary to meet the needs and achieve the goals of achieving an education.
3. An interagency focus must be developed.
4. Community ownership must be assumed. *(Interagency Task Force, 1995 pp. 15-16)*

These four points adapted by Kentucky are characterized by vision and practicality. Points one and two have a vision of the child's capability of learning and the empowerment of the client to obtain an education. Points 3 and 4 give practical direction. This is a beautiful balance of goals for which to strive and the nitty-gritty way of accomplishing those goals.

It was decided that FRCs would be located in or accessible to an elementary school in which 20 percent or more of the student body was eligible for free school meals. Income and subsequent poverty level are, of course, good indicators of need. The income level of the families in the present study is $15,000. Even taking into consideration rural living, this income figure is still quite low. However, this economic indicator is a good beginning point on which to base FRC clientele.

Noncurricular needs (Kronick & Hargis, 1990) are extremely important in the developing philosophy of FRCs. It is assumed that when physical, mental, and social needs are met, children have a better chance of school success. If a child comes to school fed, clothed, and unafraid, he/she has a better chance of learning. If the child is hungry, ill-fed, is part of violence in the home, has alcohol or drug abuse within the home, then this child has little or no chance for school success.

Family resource centers are placed in the unique position to meet both the noncurricular needs of the children as well as the curricular needs. Based on the extent of collaboration between FRCs, schools and human service agencies, success in reducing the number of at-risk students seems imminently possible. The following principles help to make the argument for school-human services collaboration:

1. The durability and stability of schools makes them an essential participant in effectively serving children and their families. Likewise, schools alone should not address all the issues faced by children and families. Partnerships between the schools and other agencies in the community should be developed.
2. Effective programs that emphasize prevention rather than costly crisis intervention are the most beneficial and productive.
3. The school should not attempt to dominate any new working relationships nor should the human service agencies. If this should occur, failure is a certainty.
4. Programs must be flexible and able to respond quickly to community-oriented crises.
5. Maximization of service accessibility and availability is best achieved through a systematic approach of coordination and cooperation involving all related parties. *Guidelines for Tennessee Family Resource Centers,* 1991, pp. 2-3.

These five points are excellent ones on which to develop and build joint programs that will meet the complex needs of the community, children, and families and, at the same time, meet the guidelines for establishing family resource centers.

Poverty alone as a standard for establishing family resource centers is sufficiently complex to require some sophisticated programs based on sound theory. But there are other guidelines for establishing family resource centers; and they include the number of single-headed households, number of teen pregnancies, number of truants, number of parents who are illiterate and, of course, others. These numbers should also be expressed in terms of the percentage of the population or as a rate.

Before the family resource center is actually started, a board of advisors is to be established by the local school board. Parents (who are in the client group being served) should comprise a majority of the advisory council.

The director of the family resource center, in conjunction with the advisory board, should do a community needs assessment very early in the development of the center. Each center works within family resource center guidelines but also relies on the findings of the needs assessment to provide services that may be unique to its service area.

It is assumed that not all necessary services will be provided by the center directly. Brokering, advocacy, and networking are part of the array of services that the center may provide. Funding for these centers in Tennessee comes from an award of up to $50,000 from the Commissioner of Education. Basic Education Program (BEP) funds may also be used. A downward spiral of one-third of the award is made each year in anticipation of the center becoming self-sufficient and fully funded by BEP funds by year four. Smrekar (1996) reports that Kentucky family resource centers are funded based on a formula that is equal to the total number of students eligible for free lunches multiplied by $200, up to a maximum grant award of $90,000 per year.

Methods

A semistructured interview was designed and carried out. The interviewer is an FRC director in an urban county in East Tennessee. This unique position allowed the interviewer to have knowledge that others would not have; at the same time, the interviewer had to be especially careful not to lead the respondents in their answers because, in a certain way, she was one of them.

The interview respondents were five directors of rural family resource centers and five clients at each of these same centers. The family resource center directors and the clients of the centers were selected based on the following criteria: (1) they had to live in a rural area, (2) four of the five centers were in the eastern part of the state, the fifth center was in the middle of the state. All participants were promised anonymity to the fullest extent possible. Neither directors nor clients appeared to be affected in any way when it came to talking with the interviewer. Detection of biases, fears and concerns is a must in qualitative research. The interviewer perceived none of these factors while interviewing the directors and the clients. However, some directors and some clients were more open than others. In regards to the clients this may be explained as much by gender of the respondent as anything else. All respondents participated voluntarily and all could withdraw from the project at anytime. The transcripts of the interviews were shared with both family resource center directors and clients for any and all comments that they might choose to make. A semistructured interview schedule was followed. Themes were looked for among clients. Themes and consistency were looked for between directors and clients. Significant differences and deviant cases were also looked for. Once the interview transcripts were typed, they were shared with respondents to see if they agreed with what was transcribed. There may be a difference between what they thought they said during the interview and what the typed transcript said when they had the opportunity to review it at a later time.

There were four readers of the transcripts, all with 2 Ph.D. and all with experience in doing qualitative research. One of the readers and the interviewer went through the data independently and found 23 themes in common. The interrater agreement on these items was considerably above 90 percent. The other three readers, also working independently, had agreement on these items over 90 percent of the time plus finding other items and themes not found by the first two readers of the interview data.

After the four readers and the interviewer had gone through the data, a meeting was held to discuss the findings from each reader. This meeting was audiotaped and then transcribed. The emergent findings from this meeting were exciting both in terms of process as well as outcome. Ideas and themes emerged from this meeting that had not occurred to any one of the readers individually. One of the most interesting findings was that Appalachian parents in this group of interviews refer to their children as "it." As the earlier quote from Coles notes these parents truly love their children; so research into this phenomenon is recommended.

Findings

The findings of this study are presented in terms of how well schools and human service agencies work together. We looked for evidence of cooperation, coordination and/or collaboration.

The role and scope of the director is crucial to the success of the family resource center. The director must be creative and client-centered. The following quote shows the importance of flexibility and the need to be able to handle the cognitive dissonance that was revealed over and over in this study:

> I just like when he comes and brings his little toys and things for them to do. They are not really toys; they are stuff you can get from your own house. You can do with the child and help them with their skills. Like one day he brought a coffee can with the top having poker chips. Julia (her daughter), (pseudonym) is really good picking them up and putting them in there with the top off. But when he put the top on with the slit in it like a piggy bank, she tried

and tried. She finally got it and was so excited. She likes that, so I got me one and she loves taking them out and putting them in that slot. He brings books by, age appropriate books. Like for Samantha (her daughter) (pseudonym), the three month old, he brings little picture books and with Julia he brings books you can read to her. (Client A, 1996)

Director A points out over and over that he is so happy in this job after having spent 28 years in the school system. He says that he gets more satisfaction from this job than any previous job. He sees that prevention and early intervention are where the action is for him and that, by the time you get kids in middle school and high school, it is much too late. This is illustrated in a quote from Client A in terms of what she is learning from Director A:

You can see where your children should be at certain ages and if there is a problem you can catch it early. Yeah, like Julia (oldest daughter) did not roll over until she was about 10 months old. And I was starting to get paranoid because they say a child should start at four months. I kept thinking come on Julia roll over. But she did other things ahead of time, so rolling over didn't bother us because she knew how to pick up food. (Client A, 1996)

This illustrates the strong personal relationship that home visits and direct service make for the family resource center director and the client.

This following is another client's experience showing the importance of the attitude of the family resource center director and how they convey to clients the importance of empowerment and self-esteem:

See when I noticed it (John's problem with A.D.D.), I didn't know how to go about doing it. But I came to school everyday and it got so they would send me notes everyday about John—we have got to find something for John. To find out more about what is going on with him. And so I would go and have meetings with the school and things kept getting worse and worse and worse. And I knew all this. But it just took me and another team, someone else from the school or something to help get me in. And once I got in with the school and they have supported me—stood with me, backed me up, then I went at it and we got John what he needed. [This something else was the FRC]. (Client D, 1996)

There is a lot of active listening that goes on. And I think if a director can do that with families, to let them know that they are doing some good things themselves, that they are really not screwed up. (Client D, 1996)

This quote from another director illustrates the importance of collaboration.

We have finally gotten a wake-up call that we cannot do it without the family unit. That it is important for us to bring the families back into the school system. One of our goals and objectives is to work with the families as kind of a collaborative person between the schools and the families. Because I think that is going to be hard for educators to turn around from years of trying to do everything themselves to suddenly involving all the parents. They [the school] don't know what to do and I look at this as a good job for the family resource centers and then to work with the at-risk population. I mean if we can do preventive things on this end and early intervention things before we have to do the treatments and the costly things at the end, like the final state custody. (Director B, 1996)

This director has certainly hit the nail on the head as to what human service delivery is all about and has summed up nicely how such key variables as collaboration, coordination, prevention, and intervention can all come together and work toward bringing together the family, the school and the community with human service providers.

And that was the beginning. And now I think because we network with them, then they remember us, and somebody calls and says hey we need some help with so and so, they say why don't you call the family resource center? Maybe they can help you. Because their only expertise is in the little area that they work whereas we network with everybody, so we know who to send them to. Like I said lots of times we are the middle man. So that was the beginning of our networking and then the other networking I think is one of our strengths. I hope that other family resource directors realize this that many times there are a lot of agency meetings, government meetings, and community meetings that educators don't have the time to go to because they are dealing with all the things that go on at the central office or whatever. It is vital for them to be there because there are a lot of agencies operating with all these facets except for education. (Director B, 1996)

This goes to the heart of the matter of curricular and noncurricular causes of at-risk children and dropouts. By seeing the need for interagency collaboration and cooperation, the issue then becomes one of how can we best deploy the troops, if you will, to deal with this immense problem.

A major finding of this research is, at least for rural centers, they might be termed family resource directors. The centers in our study were a one-person operation. Four of the five directors were women. Four had no clerical support. All but one made home visits and saw home visits as a central facet of what they did. The one who didn't make home visits said she did not because of fear. All directors were white. Three were natives to the community they were serving. Although one had lived in the area 25 years, she was considered an outsider because she was not born and raised there. The insider/outsider role had predictable costs and benefits. On the one hand an insider could be trusted; on the other hand, confidentiality could be a problem for the insider because they knew so many people in the area. Referrals were made on an informal basis by being known in the community. As one respondent said, "I remember you from being with Head Start." This same client said:

> Well I am sure that everything she does is probably available through some other resource, but a lot of these resources cost a lot of money and time and she puts her effort out through her daily work to provide these services. Where if you had to go to another service you would have to set appointments with them and you know probably spend a lot of money as far as counseling is concerned. (Client E, 1996)

This same client, in response to the question: Is there one special thing that stands out in your mind about the resource center, replied: "I think the director herself. She is very willing to help, always there when you need her, overall just puts a lot of effort into it and really cares (Client E, 1996).

Education is a fascinating variable in this study. Two directors had doctoral degrees, one a masters, one was working on a masters and one had two bachelors degrees. Formal education was valued by the directors obviously and this was socialized to clients as a virtue. One respondent equated education with survival:

> This is a real rural community and sometimes education hasn't been considered a main priority. Surviving is more important than education. And a lot of people have not been able to make the connection, that to have good survival you need to have a good education. And I think that the director has been able to make some people see education differently. (Client E, 1996)

As outlined in the FRC guidelines, each FRC was to have an advisory board. In all of the centers in this study, a board was already in place when the director came to work. The board in all instances gave support to the director but did not mandate any action. In all instances, the original grants were written by someone from the county's school system; but they made no demands on the director and simply moved aside once the director was hired and in place. Directors created and implemented the continuation grants subsequent to year one.

Networking was a key facet of life for FRC directors. Networking was stated in the guidelines but not much guidance on the "how to's" was given. Of the five programs covered in this study, one will terminate June 30, 1996. In listening to the director of this FRC, it is clear that she did not network very much. The reason for this is that she did not have enough time. As she describes her average day, one can see that she had loved the people in the area where she was and that she spent plenty of time in direct client service. What she did not do was network with fellow directors. She did network and work with the school that her program was affiliated with. This may be because she was a former school teacher in this county and is returning to the school system when her program ends.

This center will be phased out and closed by the end of the fiscal year. The reason for this is most critical to our understanding of school human service collaboration. In the county where this family resource center was located the makeup of the school board changed due to elections. The new members of the school board were opposed to such "frills" as muticultural education, family issues, and preschool enrichment and wanted a return to basics. It was the contention of the newly configured board that reading, writing and arithmetic should be the only concerns for schools in this county. Hence the center was dropped.

From a research point of view, the interesting question must be: why in this county but not in the other four? On their face all five counties seem quite similar in terms of demographics including income level, types of jobs, job availability, racial composition, major industries or lack of and recreational opportunities, etc. If this county dropped the family resource center, why didn't the other four? Or if the other four maintained and supported the family resource centers, why didn't this county? Obviously this is a research question to be pursued.

Several coalitions have evolved since the family resource centers appeared on the scene in 1993. It is difficult to tell at this point where on the cooperation-collaboration continuum they may exist, but it is easy to tell from the following quotes that previously undelivered services are now being delivered:

> One of the big groups that I worked with has been Agencies Serving Kids and that got started a few years ago by some people who saw that everybody had the same goal of helping children, but not everybody knew what every-

body else was doing. So we started getting together once a month and it can be anybody that is just concerned about children and their needs. Some of the times we have just had speakers come in and let us know some things that are going on out there. One of the things that came up that we found out about this last year was the drug and alcohol program called Reality. We had somebody come to the ASK meeting just to get information and everybody that was there just said yes we need to do this in Smith County. (Director C, 1996)

To further illustrate the cooperative and collaborative modes in which the family resource centers are working and bringing other agencies together is the following quote regarding services that are incomplete and how the FRC helped to make the services complete:

We found out that there are a lot of places that will pay for glasses and for some other needs of the kids; but they would not pay for the testing, for hearing tests and eye tests. So the Salvation Army decided that they would pay for that. So we have had some kids who have been able to get some exams done through the Salvation Army. And one of the things that came up but it was after the school year had already started, so one of the units has already decided what their back-to-school program would be next year. There was also a member of the health department and she said as kids were coming through getting ready for kindergarten they had to have their physicals. She saw how many kids did not have underwear. And of course already being in the school year it was too late to go back and figure out who those were. She would be able to tell up front who those were and then through the school we can find some others. She will be able to target a whole lot of them at that point. So together we have been able to come up with some things and we are checking with parents to find out what their needs are rather than everybody else sitting back and dictating. (Director C, 1996)

This illustrates that many of these clients are operating at a survival level. If you look at them in a hierarchy-of-needs framework, you must take care of primary needs like food, shelter, and clothing and, in this case, underwear, before you can move on to the next level. This may explain why in human services so often services are offered that clients will not take advantage of. It is hard to be concerned about a GED degree when your kids don't have underwear.

To further illustrate how networking is being done by these rural family resource directors, the following quote, again from Director C, is instructive:

And that therapist also attends the ASK meetings, so I know that once a month I can go in with my list of questions and say: "Okay, this is a child that ...., this is the scenario; tell me what to do. So that has been—I hit her up every month and she knows I am going to be there.

In responding to the question, are you aware of any goal that the state has set out for all family resource centers to work towards, Director C says:

> I guess more networking so that there are other agencies involved; we are not just here on our own, doing our own thing. There are a lot of agencies, organizations, churches, individuals who have been involved with us to work with families. (Director C, 1996)

As mentioned earlier, networking was stressed by the state as a major goal; but not much direction was given to the FRC on how to go about doing it. The above quote shows that this director had pretty good insight as to what networking was all about.

Yet another voice is heard from Director C:

> Social skills are a biggy! There are so many behavioral problems with the children and some of that just comes up with parents not knowing a different way to handle some issues or being too tired to deal with it. And that, in a home visit, is very easy to see!

Here we see the importance of the home visit, the family resource director and the openness of the parents. This particular quote is very powerful and says a great deal as to the collaborative, cooperative venture of the family resource center folks, the other human service agencies, and the community (in this case the family).

The physical location of the FRCs was adjacent to or part of a school. The center seemed to have the best of both worlds in that they maintained privacy for their clients by having their own separate entrances, yet at the same time they could use secretarial help from the school. Most centers were short-handed, to put it mildly, when it came to secretarial help; so help from the school was greatly appreciated. Of the two programs that had secretarial help, one used a secretary more as a case aid in making home visits, than as a typist. The other director did not make home visits and used the secretary in a more traditional manner. To further elucidate on this point, hear what the following client has to say about the director and support staff for the director.

> Well, usually I get help upon request. But my opinion about it, I think Director D could use an assistant to help her out. I think it would help a lot. It would help her to .... she does a great job as is, but I think she could do a lot more, if she had an assistant here to help her do paperwork or whatever. (Client D, 1996)

The size and amenities of the FRC's offices are small and sparse. Most were no larger than a standard-sized room. This, of course, is of little consequence to those directors who center their activities around home visits. As Smrekar (1996) p. 10, found from one of her respondents:

> If I am part of the building, I am part of the problem. I don't know what coordinators are doing if they are not making home visits. I need to know what the family needs are, not just hear about them. It is a hands-on approach. My job is to build trust and to offer something to people so that they will come to us. I am not a guidance counselor. I am not a social worker. I am not here to judge but to help.
>
> But I do most of my work outside of the office; this is just kind of a home base for me. I do see a few clients in here but it is not a whole lot. Most of mine is done outside in the homes and my classes—that sort of thing, not in the center. (Director D, 1996)

Another director had this to say,

> We are located at the high school and have basically two small rooms. One serves as a classroom and office counseling area. The other is a very small office with a computer and telephone, our communications area. Basically I am in and out of the office and a lot of the things that I do are off campus at the other schools for elementary school, middle school and a high school in classrooms. So mostly activities do not go on in the center itself. (Director E, 1996)

This shows a strong element of something existing somewhere between cooperation and collaboration and also illustrates the fact that the director is out of the office more than in the office. It also illustrates the concept of the center as director and the director as Center.

Advocacy and brokering are two other driving forces of the FRC. Advocacy was found to be a strong force for these directors of the rural centers. The following quotes from one of the clients illustrates the importance of advocacy and brokering:

> I think the fact that we don't have any resources, Director B is in a position to be able to connect to people having the type of financial troubles that if they need help with lights or food or something like that, she knows who to connect them to. (Client B, 1996)

In addition, Smrekar (1996) found that:

> The center coordinator sits at her executive-style desk only when using the telephone; she uses the round table for all other business to avoid the sitting at the head of the table image of authority. I don't want our parents to feel challenged; I want them to feel like we are their advocates. (p. 8)

A stereotype of rural areas is that there just isn't much to do there. This was brought up by two respondents and leads to concrete collaborative services that could be provided in these rural areas. As Director D says:

> Not a lot [of recreational] activities are offered here. We have the city park, that is about the only thing, and the community center. The community center is not used a whole lot because it costs, I think, a dollar to get in and a lot of families are not close to it. It is in the middle of town but it is just not used a whole lot. We are very lacking as far as recreational activities. I think especially the teenagers. They are trying to get bowling started right now and I know that lots of teenagers have absolutely nothing to do. (Director D, 1966)

There are similarities between rural and urban areas, but there are unique qualities to the rural Appalachian South. Given the importance of family, language, and communication, activities that are centered around these three variables might lead to curtailing problems such as alcohol and drug abuse, violence, poor school performance, and problems arising from boredom. Having something to do would also cut down on migration from the area.

Activities that exist in rural areas are too often centered on the tourist and not on the local resident. Dollywood, High Hampton Inn, and the fascinations of Pigeon Forge and Gatlinburg are too often out of the price range of local children.

Affordable recreational activities are a must for these areas. Of course, the mountains, hiking, and fishing are always there and affordable, but more can and should be done. It has been suggested that the best thing that Appalachians can do is to move away—all of them. This was shared with me by Mr. Jim Sessions, Director of Highlander Research Center, New Market, Tennesseee, when he was director of the Congress of Religion in Appalachia. This conversation was between a Washington bureaucrat and Mr. Sessions in late 1992 (Personal communication, Kronick & Sessions).

Conclusions

What have we learned from all of this?

1. Appalachia was not the ideal place for family resource centers. Given the cultural description that is offered in this chapter, it can be seen that Appalachia, particularly its rural parts, is not the ideal place for rural family resource centers to be developed and implemented.

2. That the family resource center in the rural Appalachian South translates into the rural family resource director. The importance of the individual in this position cannot be overestimated. The individual directors that were followed and studied over the time period of this study revealed that in the two to three years that they had been on the job they had become very involved in what they were doing. Even though they found time for pursuing advanced degrees, they also found time, with one exception, to make home visits, to network, to attend regional and national conferences and to be deeply involved in the lives of the clients that they were serving in the rural Appalachian South.

3. Direct service, home visits, and networking are important. Catchwords, trends, and other new fads fade in and out of human services; but some of the old tried-and-true techniques of human service work emerge as critically important for at-risk youth in the rural Appalachian South. Direct service is something that still cannot be replaced. It was found that case management was just not something that was done very often in these centers or by these directors; however, direct service and home visits were. The home visit was almost the core of what the family resource center director did. They learned what was going on in people's lives by making a home visit. They got involved in direct service and then, when appropriate, made referrals. Networking was also something that was found to be of critical importance for the survival of the family resource director.

4. Education was equated with survival and survival with education. It was noted that education may not have a very high value in the rural Appalachian South; but in this instance, we are beginning to see the rise in importance of education in this region. As one client put it, "I want something better for my children than what I had. I don't want them to have to work in the fields." (Client B, 1996)

5. Cooperation, coordination, and collaboration can be done. Instance after instance in this study reflected that cooperation, coordination, and collaboration were, in fact, being done. People saw the need to work together and found that if working together did not occur, they were surely on the road to failure.

6. As one of the clients so eloquently put it, "It is worse to start up a program and then leave than to never start up at all." This is a given in almost any introduction to human service textbook. Yet here we

hear from a client about how often programs have come in, giving them hope, and then have left. This is a byword that we must live by, if we are going in, we need to stay for the long haul.

7. Theory, practice, and policy all ran together. Even though we started this chapter with an elaboration of limitations of colocation of services, it has been our attempt to show that the colocation of services can and will work and that it is the way to go for at-risk kids and, in this case, rural at-risk kids. Hence policy can be established in which family resource centers play a middle-man role between the school and the community.

It may be that in 1998, as it comes to the issue of at-risk students, at-risk families, and at-risk culture in society, that we may have to go one step at a time. Large massive programs that look at the issue as being so mammoth may miss some very important points. Possibly these family resource centers in the rural Appalachian South are an avenue to be pursued more fully. Client B sums up the healthy marriage, if you will, of collaboration, cooperation, and coordination of services in the rural Appalachian South, showing that this can be done, that colocation of services can occur successfully, and that we are making a difference at least in one person's life.

> Just because we are rural doesn't mean you know maybe we don't have quite the level of violence and stuff like that puts the inner cities in a crisis but I think we are losing a lot of people. There are a lot of really intelligent people that are still living like they did fifty years ago. And the mentality that goes along with it as far as education is unimportant but children that are brilliant. And I think this resource center can really open some eyes you know. Maybe I cannot get much past a factory job but my child really can! And here somebody is saying: yes, if you encourage them to do their homework, maybe they won't have to live from week to week. And I would hate to see all that go away just because Washington pulls the funding.

Chapter 16

WHAT HAS TRANSPIRED FROM 1990 TO 1998

In writing the second edition of *Dropouts: Who drops out and why and the recommended action*, we must ask ourselves what has happened in the past seven years since our initial publication with Charles C Thomas, Publisher. What, if any, progress has been made in lowering the dropout rate? What successes have been recorded in keeping young children out of the fast track of the at-risk thoroughfare?

Since 1990, monies have been appropriated from all levels of government. Have these allocations made any difference? Is it possible that the prospects for at-risk youth have actually gotten worse? The answer to these questions as always lies in the indicators used. Recent reports from the federal government show a decline in the dropout rate. But other indicators such as violent crime show a rise in at-risk status.

The term "at-risk" initially referred to physical symptoms such as deafness or blindness. The term today is more likely to refer to a broad spectrum of behavior starting with school-based behavior. Juvenile violence is one area where at-risk status tends to flow into. Students not in school appear to have a higher risk of being a perpetrator or a victim, though causality is not being argued here. In 1980, juveniles were murdered at a rate of five per day. By 1994, the rate was seven per day, and most were 15 to 17 years of age (Diiulio, 1996). In 1994, 2.7 million juveniles were arrested, more than a third of them under 15. Males, 14 to 24 years of age, were only 8 percent of the population but they made up more than 25 percent of all homicide victims, and 30 percent of all the offenders (Diiulio, 1996). Children of color figure even more disproportionately as victims and offenders. The saddest part of all of this is that these young people present a profile of lack of remorse, defiance, sulleness, and anger. A recent tragedy in rural East Tennessee involved the killing of a young couple and their 6-year-old daughter, miraculously their 2-year-old son survived, at a rest stop on Interstate 81. The accused in this case range in age from 14 to 22. These young people are described as disenchanted, disinterested, and seeing the world as coming to an end. One of the young ladies was married in black, her bridesmaids wore dog collars and chains. The films of these folks reflects the description presented above of lack of remorse, disenchantment, etc. They fit what James Q. Wilson terms a feral presocial being, cited in Diiulio (1996).

We must acknowledge that most teenage predators begin as severely high-risk children. An abundance of scholarly evidence shows that antisocial and delinquent tendencies emerge early in the lives of neglected, abused and unloved youngsters often by age 9 (Mark Fleisher cited in the Diiulio, 1996).

One of the authors (Kronick) takes at-risk high school students to visit prisons. The goal is never to scare these young people. They already know someone who is in this prison, a parent friend, or relative.

As stated elsewhere, Kronick and Hargis (1990), Kronick (1997), and *Kids Count* (1995), the overall well-being of children is measured and evaluated in many different ways leading to various different conclusions. The state of the union on dropouts is that overall matters haven't improved much over the past seven years and there is still a great deal of work to do to cut the dropout rate and improve the general well-being of children.

Some highlights that have occurred since 1990, include Hillary Rodham Clinton's *It Takes a Village,* Kronick's explication of the school as a human service agency, the development of family resource centers, and the most recent addition of *Kids Count.*

Clinton's theories on the notion that child-raising is everyone's concern is nothing new. It appears at a time when a sense of community in America is dearly lacking and sorely needed. Partisan politics aside Clinton's book pushes hard for the need for community.

In the *Good Society,* a follow-up to *Habits of the Heart* (Bellah et., al, 1985), once again strongly advocate a communitarian paradigm for American society. They give a strong exegesis on needed social science style as well as an everyday approach to living that is based on individuals meeting their needs through institutions and organizations. They make a strong point that institutions and organizations are not the same. Their strongest point is linking the individual to organizations to reach a higher level of abstraction. As an example, Bellah et

al. (1991) choose "greening" or recycling as an example. They make
the point that individuals may recycle on their own and that institutions may support recycling but the jump to prevention and not pol-
luting in various forms requires a powerful sense of community.

The analogy holds for dropouts and dropout prevention. The first
line of attack was to look for causes of dropping out within the individual. Several texts including our own had found individual factors
such as race, gender, IQ, etc. that are correlated with dropping out.
Subsequently the organization, the school, was studied to find its contribution to early school leaving. Now following the lead of Bellah et
al. (1991), the crucial link between the individual and the institution
must be studied and tied to the broader social fabric in reducing the
dropout rate. This would include political, economic, and social variables.

Kronick (1997) argues strongly that the school become a human
service agency. The school in this scenario builds on the foundation
provided by Dryfoos (1994). The school now becomes a front bumper
for human service delivery to the student and his or her family. The
school and human services collaborate in this scenario. Collaboration
means that the school and human services share a common set of values and work together to achieve them. This model goes beyond
cooperation where organizations work together but have their own set
of values rather than sharing a common set of values. This collaborative model relies heavily on open communication. There is a vital
need to do away with turfism under this model. Flexibility is a key
organizational style. Doing business as usual or "if it ain't broke don't
fix it;" or no; or no we can't do that; are not part of this system. At-risk
becomes at-promise.

The school is a good parent in this paradigm. The school is open
12 months a year and well beyond the hours of the school day.
Learning goes on from 7:00 A.M. until 2:00 A.M. Human service workers including law enforcement, counseling, welfare, and health have
offices in the school. The school is a centrifugal force for the community. It will draw its constituents from the community it serves and
give them good things. Arts and crafts, basketball at midnight, family
discussion groups, etc. will be facilitated by school-human service personnel at the school building.

A movement designed to increase school success for at-risk students is family resource centers. These centers were established in

Kentucky as a response to demands made by the federal government. These centers are discussed fully in our new edition and data are presented from an ongoing study of rural centers in a southeastern state.

Whether or not these centers reduce the number of dropouts cannot yet be determined. However, initial findings suggest that they do. Other findings such as those of Smrekar (1996) reflect that school/parent interaction does not increase because of center involvement. As shown in our new chapter, the centers are successful on many other fronts.

The 1995 edition of *Kids Count* reflects trends of the past six years. The southeastern part of the United States ranks in the lowest sector on almost all indicators of child well-being. In Tennessee, the number of single parent families is skyrocketing due to one of the nation's highest divorce rates, third in the nation, and an incredibly high number of births to single mothers. This trend of single-parent families as illustrated so strongly in Tennessee is also a national trend according to *Kids Count*. They state that the trend towards father absence is not a good thing for most of the children affected by it; and second, the share of children and mother-only families is increasing dramatically. The *Kids Count* document goes on to say more than anything else changes in family structure appear to be linked to the changes in labor force experience for males. Despite cultural shifts in the roles of men and women over the past few decades being the significant breadwinner remains a key element of fatherhood in America.

Kids Count goes on to say that the rapid increase in violent crime and unmarried teenage childbearing reflects the growing problems faced by adolescents making the transition from childhood to adulthood. Is it any wonder that the noncurricular effects on school dropouts is as gigantic as it is?

At the same time that we are seeing the problems of adolescents, we are also seeing problems for those who are born as low birth weight babies. *Kids Count* presents information that those infants born at five and a half pounds or less have a high probability of experiencing developmental problems. Therefore, the percent of low birth weight babies reflects a group of children that are likely to have problems as they move through developmental growth stages and enter school.

In looking at risk status the early years are, of course, of utmost importance. The first year is by far the most important in brain development. During this early development, play and trauma are to be singled out for special importance. Hands-on parenting including play and nurturance gives the child a leg up on healthy development. The importance of nurturance is discussed in the time-honored study of Harlow's monkeys. Hungry baby monkeys went to a cloth wrapped wire monkey without food rather than a wire monkey with food. As important as nurturing parenting is, so too, are the effects of bad parenting where abuse and trauma are present. Trauma inflicted on a child before the age of three is wired into the child's brain. An abused child sitting in a classroom is hearing, seeing and sensing very different things from the teacher than a healthy child is. This is due to the wiring in the brain that has been a result of this abuse. Nature and nurture are thus both working together here.

It is important that both the school and human service agencies work together to help the young at-risk child. Through repeated positive experiences, the impact of early trauma may be lessened. When schools and human service agencies work together prevention of this abuse is often possible. Family resource centers presented in this text are a step in the right direction of prevention and early intervention for abuse and trauma.

The idea of children being born as a blank slate is no longer viable, especially for the many children who are at risk for the later behavior of school failure, violence, and lack of participation in American culture to their fullest possibilities.

REFERENCES

Agee, J. (1960). *Let us now praise famous men*. New York: Houghton Mifflin.

Agnew, R. (1985). Social control theory and delinquency: A longitudinal test. *Criminology, 23* (1).

Apicella, R. *Perceptions of why migrant students drop out of school and what can be done to encourage them to graduate*. Oneonta NY: SUNY at Oneonta, 1985.

Archibald, D. A., & Newman, F. M. (1988). *Beyond standardized testing: Assessing authentic academic achievement in the secondary school*. Reston: National Association of Secondary School Principals.

Argyris, C. (1957). Personality and organization. New York: Harper & Row.

Bachman, G. et al. (1972). Dropping out is a symptom, *Education Digest, 37* 1-5.

Barker, R., & Gump, P (1964). *Big school small school*. Stanford, CA: Stanford University Press.

Beder, H. H. *Adult literacy: Issues for policy and practice*. Malabar, FL: Krieger, 1991.

Bellah, R., et al. (1985). *Habits of the heart*. Berkley,CA: University of California Press.

Bellah, R., et al. (1991). *The good Society*. Berkley, CA: University of California Press.

Bertoglio, J (1985). *Current strengths in Chapter One and approaches to resolving presistent problems*. A compilation of papers on the 20th anniversary of the Elementary and Secondary Education Act of 1985, Subcommittee on Elementary, Secondary, and Vocational Education (Serial Number 99D). Washington, D.C.: United States Government Printing Office.

Best, B. (1986). *The great Appalachian sperm bank & other writings*. Berea, KY. Kentucky Imprints.

Bettis, E. A.(1964). *Foundation of reading instruction*. New York: American Book.

Bolman, L., & Deal, T. (1991). *Reframing organizations*. San Francisco: Jossey-Bass.

Boshier, R. W. Educational Participation and Dropout: A Theoretical Model. *Adult Education* 1973, *23*, 255-282.

Brill, N. (1976). *Teamwork: Working together in the human services*. Philadelphia: J.B. Lippincott Company.

Butchcart, R. E. (1986). *Dropout prevention through alternative high schools: A study of* the *national experience*. Elmira, New York: Elmira Board of Cooperative Educational Services, 1-26.

Caldwell, C. (1970). Social science as ammunition. *Psychology Today,* 38-41.

Carrillo, L. W. (1964) *Informal Reading - Readiness Experiences*. San Francisco: Chandler.

Catterall, J. S. (1986). School dropouts. *Policy Prospects*. Charleston, WV: Appalachian Educational Laboratory.

Caudill, H. (1963). *Night comes to the Cumberlands*. San Francisco: Jossey-Bass.

Celebreeze, A. J. (1982). *Hispanic access to postsecondary education*. Paper presented to the United States Congress Subcommittee on Postsecondary Education of the House Committee on Education and Labor.

Cervantes, L. (1965). *The dropout: Causes and cures.* Ann Arbor, MI: The University of Michigan Press.

Clinton, H. (1996). *It takes a Village.* New York: Simon & Schuster.

Cloward, R. A., & Ohlin, L. E. (1960). *Delinquency and opportunity.* New York: Free Press of Glencoe.

Cohen, A. K. (1955). *Delinquent boys.* New York: Free Press of Glencoe.

Coleman J., Campbell, E. Q., & Hobson, C. J. (1966). *Equality of educational opportunity.* Washington, D.C.: United States Printing Office.

Coles, R. (1967). *Migrants, sharecroppers, and mountaineers: Volutne II of children of crisis.* Boston, MA: Little, Brown, & Company.

Conant, J. B. (1961). *Slums and suburbs.* New York: McGraw-Hill.

Cranston-Gingras, A., Platt, J.; Flores, Y., Doone, P. & Martinez, Y. *Voices from the field: What research with farnworker children and youth adult is telling us.* Paper presented at the 1993 National Conference on Migrant and Seasonal Farmworkers, Denver, CO, April 13, 1993.

Cressey, D. (1961). *The prison: Studies in institutional organization and change.* New York: Holt, Rinehart, & Winston.

Crowson, R., & Boyd, W. (1996). Structure & strategies toward an understanding of alternative models for coordinated childrens services. In J. Cibulka, & W. Kriterk. (Eds..), *Coordination among schools, families & communities.* pp. 137-172. Albany: State University of New York Press.

Cureton, W. L. (1971). The history of grading practices. *NCME, 2,* 1-8.

Dale, E. (1969). *Management: Theory and practice.* New York: McGraw-Hill.

Diiulio, J. (1996). Stop crime before it starts. NY: *New York Times* (July 31).

Dryfoos, J. (1994). *Full service schools.* San Francisco, CA: Jossey-Bass.

Elliott, D. et al. (1967). Capable dropouts in the milieu of high school. *Journal of Educational Research, 60,* 180-186.

Elliott, D., & Voss, H. (1974). *Delinquency and dropouts.* Lexington, MA: Lexington Books.

Evans, F. B. (1976). What research says about grading. In S. B. Simon & J. A. Ballanca (Eds.), *Degrading the grading myths: A primer of alternatives to grades and marks* (pp. 30-50). Washington: Association for Supervision and Curriculum Development. *Federal Aid Report,* Bureau of Business, Practice, Incorporated. Waterford, CT: Croft-Nei.

Fne, M. *Why urban adolescents drop into and out of public schools.* Teachers College Record, 1986, 97, 393-409.

Fingeret, H. *North Carolina ABE instructional program evaluation.* Raleigh, N.C.: Dept. of Adult and Community College Education, 1985.

Ford, W.D. *Migrant education: A consolidated view.* A special report of the Education Commission of the United States. Denver, CO.

Fordham, S., & Ogbu, J. U. Black students' school success: Coping with the 'burden' of acting white'. *Urban Review,* 1986, *18,* 176-206.

Forell, E. R. (1985). The case for conservative reader placement. *The Reading Teacher, 38,* 875-862.

Gibson M. *Variability in immigrant students' school performance: The U.S. case.* American Education Research Association-Division G The Social Context of Education Newsletter. Winter, 1993.

Gickling, E. E., & Thompson, V. (1985). A personal view of curriculum-based assessment. *Exceptional Children, 52,* 205-218.

Giroux, H. *Theory and resistance in education.* South Hadley, MA: Begin &.Garvey, 1983.

Glasser, W. (1971). *The effect of school failure on the life of a child.* Washington: National Association of Elementary School Principals.

Glasser, W. (1986). *Control theory in the classroom.* New York: Harper & Row.

Glueck, S., & Glueck, E. (1968). *Delinquent and non-delinquents in perspective.* Cambridge: Harvard University Press.

Goetz, J., & LeCompte, M. (1984). *Ethnography and qualitative design in educational research.* Orlando, FL: Academic Press.

Goffman, E. (1961). *Asylums* Garden City, NY: Doubleday.

Gove, W. (1974). Individual resources and mental hospitalization: A comparison and evaluation of the societal reaction and psychiatric perspectives. *American Sociological Review, 39.*

Grant, U.S. (1885). *Personal memoirs of U.S. Grant, Vol 1.* New York: Charles L.Webster.

Grimes, L.(1981). Learned helplessness and attribution theory: Redefining children's learning problems. *Learning Disability Quarterly, 4,* 91-100. *Guidelines for Tennessee Family Resource Centers.*

Hahn, A. (1987). Reaching out to America's dropouts. What to do. *Phi Delta Kappan* 256-263.

Haplin, A., & Croft, D. (1963). *The organizational climate of schools.* Midwest Administration Center. Chicago: University of Chicago.

Hargis, C. (1987). *Curriculum based assessment: A primer.* Springfield, IL: Charles C Thomas.

Hargis, C. (1982). *Teaching reading to handicapped children.* Denver: Love.

Harrington, M. (1963). *The other America.* Baltimore, MD: Penguin.

Hawhee, Eddie, Assessment of Student Attitudes–Chestnut Ridge Learning Center, January 1993.

Hayes, E. R. Hispanic Adults and ESL Programs: Barrier to Participation. *TESOL Quarterly. 1989 23,* (1) 13-21.

Headlee, Edward, & Dutton, Garry, "Transforming Vo-Tech in London County," *TSBA Journal, April 1993,* pp. 17-19.

Hintz, J. *Poverty, prejudice, power, politics: Migrants speak about their lives* Columbus, OH: Avonelle Associations Publishers, 1961.

Hirschi, T. (1969). *Causes of delinquency.* Beverly Hills, CA: University of California Press.

Hodgkinson, H. L. *All one system: Demographics of education through graduate school.* Institute of Education Leadership, Inc. 1985.

Jansky, J., & de Hirsch, K. (1972). *Preventing reading failure: Prediction, diagnosis, intervention.* New York: Harper & Row.

Jenkins, J. R., & Pany, D. (1978). Standardized achievement tests: How useful for special education? *Exceptional Children, 44,* 448-453.

Jibrell, S. (1987). *Dropouts: A national migrant perspective.* Paper presented at the National Symposium on Achievement and Challenges and Migrant Education, The National Governors Conference.

Johnson, F. C. (1985). *Migrant students at the secondary level: Issues and opportunities for change.* Washington, D.C.: National Institute of Education.

Jones, W. (1977). The impact on society of youth who drop out or are undereducated. *Educational Leadership,* 34, 411-416

Kaplan, J., & Luck, E. (1977). The dropout phenomenon as a social problem. *Educational Forum, 42* (40), 41-56.

Kauffman, J. M. (1989). *Characteristics of behavior disorders of children and youth* (4th ed.). Columbus, OH: Merrill..

Kerr, M. M., & Zigmond, N. (1986). What do high school teachers want? A study of expectations and standards. *Education & Treatment of children. 9,* 239-249.

Kids Count (1995). *Kids count data book.* Baltimore, MA: Annie E. Casey Foundation.

King-Stoops, J. B. *Migrant education: Teaching the wandering ones.* Bloomington, IN: Phi Delta Kappa Educational Foundation, 1980.2

Kronick R. (Ed) (1997). *At risk youth: Theory, practice and reform.* New York: Garland.

Kronick, R. & Hargis, C. (1990). *Dropouts: Who drops out and why and the recommended action.* Springfield, IL. Charles C Thomas.

Kronick, R. F. (1972). The impact of organizational climate on academic performance. *The Southern Journal of Educational Research,* 169-188.

Kunisawa, F. (1987). *A nation in crisis: The dropout dilemnta.* National Education Association, 61-65.

Kutner, L. (1989, March 23). Parent & child: In athletics, it doesn't matter whether youngsters win or lose; it's how they learn to play. *The New York Times.*

Lanier, N. W. (1986). *Educational excellence and potential dropouts. Theory, research, and policy implications.* Charleston, WV: Appalachian Educational Laboratory.

Larsen, P., & Shertzer, B. (1987). The high school dropout: Everybody's problem? *The School Counselor,* 163-169.

Lawrence, P. R., & Lorsch, J. (1967) *Organizational and environment.* Cambridge, MA: Harvard University Press.

Lawson, R. & Anderson, P. (1996). Community based schools as medical education reform. In Harris, H. & Maloney D. *Human Services-Contemporary Issues & Trends.* pp. 161-172. Boston: Allyn & Bacon.

Leiter, J., & Brown, J. S. (1985). Determinants of elementary school grading. *Sociology of Education,* 58, 166-180.

Lewis, T. A., & Lewis, M. D. (1983). *Management of human service programs.* Monterey. CA: Brook & Cole.

Lloyd, D.N. (1978). Prediction of school failure from third grade data. *Educational & Psylchological Measurement, 38.*

Mann, D. (1986). Can we help dropout: Thinking about the undoable. *Teachers College Record, 87,* 307-323.

Marx, K. Capitol. (1969) *Moscow:* Progress.

McLeod, J. (1987) *Ain't no makin it: leveled spirations in a low- income neighborhood.* Boulder, CO: Westview.

McPherson, J. M. (1988). *Battle cry of freedom: The civil war era.* New York: Ballantine.

Melaville, A. & Blank, M. (1993). *Together we can. A guide for crafting a profamily system of education & human services.* Washington, D.C. vs. Dept. of Education & U.S. Dept. of Health & Human Services.

Merton, R. (1957). *Social theory and social structure.* New York: Free Press.

Milton, O., Pollio, H. R., & Eison, J. A. (1986). *Making sense of college grades.* San Francisco: Jossey-Bass.

Moos, R. (1970) Deferential effects of the social climates of correctional institutions. *Journal of Research in Crime & Delinquency, 7,* 71-82.

Murphy, G., & Likert, R. (1937). *Public opinion and the individual.* New York: Harper & Row.

National Council of La Raza. *Hispanic education: A statistical portrait.* Washington, DC: National Council of La Raza Publications, 1990.

Natriello, G. et al. (1986). Taking stock: Renewing our research agenda on the causes and consequences of dropping out. *Teachers Cottage Record, 87,* 430-440

NEA. (1974). *Evaluation and reporting of student achievement.* Washington: Author.

Ogbu, J. U. Minorities status and literacy In comparative perspectives *Daedulus. 1990, 19, (2),* 141-168.

Orr, M. T. (1987). *Keeping students in school.* San Francisco: Jossey-Bass.

Ouchi. W. (1982). *Theory Z: How American business can meet the Japanese challenge.* New York: Avon.

Parsons, T. (1965). Youth in the context of American society. In Erik Erikson, *The challenge of youth.* Garden City, N Y.: Anchor.

Peng, S. (1985). *High school dropouts: A national concern.* Washington, D.C.: National Center for Educational Statistics, 1-16.

Peng, S. & Takai, R. (1983), *High school dropouts: Descriptive information from high school and beyond.* Washington, D.C.: National Center for Educational Statistics, 1-9.

Pollio, H. R. (1984). What students think about and do in college lecture classes (Teaching-Learning Issues No. 53). Knoxville: Learning Research Center, The University of Tennessee.

Prewitt-Diaz, J. O., Trotter, R. T. & Rivera V. A. *The effects of migration on children: An ethnographic study.* PA: Center de Estudios Sabre La Migracion, 1990.

Quigley, A.B. Hidden Logic: Reproduction and Resistance in Adult Literacy and Basic Education. *Adult Education Quarterly. 199040,* 103-115.

Quigley, A.B. Looking Back in Anger: The Influences of Schooling on Illiterate Adults.Unpublished manuscript. 1991.

Quigley, A. *Resistance, Reluctance, and Persistence: Schooling and its Effect on Adult Literacy.* Paper presented at the Adult Education Research Conference. Saskatchewan, Canada. 1992.

Raywid, M. A. (1984). Synthesis of research on schools of choice. *Educational Leadership, 41,* 70-78.

Resnick, L. B. (1987). The 1987 presidential address: Learning in school and out. *Educational Researcher, 16,* 13-20.

Rokeach, M. (1960). *The open and closed mind.* New York: Basic Books.

Rosenhahn, D. M. (1973). On being sane in insane places. *Science, 179,* 250-258.

Rosenshine, B. V., & Berliner, D. C. (1978). Academic engaged time. *British Journal of Teacher Education, 4,* 3-16.

Rotter, J. (1975). Some problems and misconceptions related to the construct of internal versus external control of reinforcement. *Journal of Counseling and Clinical Psychology, 43,* 56-67.

Rumberger, R. (1983). Dropping out of high school: The influence of race, sex, and family background. *American Educational Research Journal, 20,* 199-220.

Ryan, W. (1971). *Blaming the victim.* New York: Vintage Books.

Scheff, T. (1974). A labeling theory of mental illness. *American Sociological Review, 39.*

Schreiber, D. (Ed.). (1964). *Guidance and the school dropout.* Washington, D.C.: National Education Association.

Schur, E. (1971). *Labeling deviant behavior.* New York: Harper & Row, Inc.

Scott, M. B., & Lyman, S. M. (1970). Accounts, deviance, and social order. In J.D. Douglas (Ed.), *Deviance and respectability: The social construction of moral meanings.* New York: Basic Books.

Seeman, M. *Annual Review of sociology, 1975, 1,*91-123.

Sewell, T. et al. (1981). High school dropout: Psychological, academic, and vocational factors. *Urban Educational, 16,* 65-70.

Shriner, J., & Salvia, J. (1988). Chronic noncorrespondence between elementary math curricula and arithmetic tests. *Exceptional Children 55,* 240-248.

Simon, S. B., & Bellanca, J. A. (Eds.). (1976). *Degrading the grading myths: A primer of alternatives to grades and marks.* Washington: Association for Supervision and Curriculum Development.

Skinner, B. F. (1972). Teaching: The arrangement of contingencies under which something is taught. In N. G. Haring & A. H. Hayden (Eds.), *Improvement of Instruction.* Seattle: Special Child.

Slavin, R. E. (1983). When does cooperative learning improve student achievement? *Psychological Bulletin, 94,* 429-455.

Slavin, R. E. (1987). A theory of school and classroom organization. *Educational Psychologist, 22,* 889-108.

Smith, A. Z., & Dobbin, J. E. (1960). Marks and marking systems. In C. W. Harris (Ed.), *The encyclopedia of educational research* (pp. 783-791). New York: Macmillan.

Smrekar, C. (1996). The Kentucky family resource centers: The challenges of remaking family school interactions. pp. 3-37. In J. Cibulka & W. Kritek. *Coordination among Schools, Families & Communities.* Albany: State University of New York Press.

Sofer, C. (1972). *Organizations in theory and practice.* New York: Basic Books.

Stanovich, K. E. (1986). Matthew effects in reading: Some consequences of individual differences in the acquisition of literacy. *Reading Research Quarterly, 21,* 360-407.

Stevens, R. J., Madden, N. A., Slavin, R. E., & Farnish, A. M. (1987). Cooperative integrated reading and composition: Two field experiments. *Reading Research Quarterly, 22,* 433-454.

Stinchcombe, A. (1964). *Rebellion in a high school.* Chicago: Quadrangle Books.

Stinnett, C. (1996). Family resource centers in rural East Tennessee. Unpublished doctoral dissertation, University of Tennessee, Knoxville.

Stone, B., Cundick, B. P., & Swanson, D. (1988). Special education screening system: Group achievement test. *Exceptional Children, 55,* 71-75.

Sutherland, E. (1947). *Principles of criminology (4th ed.).* Philadelphia: J. B. Lippincott.

Sutherland, E. H., & Cressey, D. R. (1966). *Principles of criminology.* Philadelphia: J. B Lippincott & Co.

Tennessee Code Annotated. (1989). Nashville, TN: Tennessee State Government.

Thaller, E. (1996).Appalachian Culture & Schooling. pp. In R. Kronick, *At Risk Youth: Theory, Practices Reform.* New York: Garland Press.

Thomas, W. I. (1967). *The unadjusted girl.* New York: Harper & Row.

Thornberry, T., Moore, N., & Christenson, R. L. (1985). The effects of dropping out of high school on subsequent criminal behavior. *Criminologly, 23* (1), 3-18.

Topping, K. (1988). *The peer tutoring handbook: Promoting cooperative learning.* Bechenham, Kent: Croom Helm.

Topping, K. (1989). Peer tutoring and paired reading: Combining two powerful techniques. *The Reading Teacher, 42,* 488-494.

Tucker, J. A. (1985). Curriculum-based assessment: An introduction. *Exceptional Children, 52,* 199-204.

Uttero, D. A. (1988). Activating comprehension through cooperative learning. *The Reading Teacher 41,* 390-395.

Valentin, T. & Darkenwald, G. G. Deterrents to Participation in Adult Education: Profiles of Potential Learners. *Adult Education Quarterly, 1990, 41,* (1), 29-42.

Velazquez, L.C. Migrant Adults' Perceptions of Schooling, Learning, and Education. Unpublished doctoral dissertation, College of Education, University of Tennessee, 1993.

Warner, L., & DeFleur, M (1969). Attitudes as an interactional concept: Social constraint and social distance of intervening variables between attitudes and action. *American Sociological Review, 34,153-170.*

Weber, M. (1958). *Essays in sociology.* Translated, edited, and with an introduction by H. H. Gerth & C. W. Mills, New York: Oxford University Press.

Wehlage, G. et al. (1986). Dropping out: How much do schools contribute to the problems? *Teachers College Record, 87,* 374-392.

Wigginton, E. (1972). *Foxfire.* Garden City, NY: Anchor-Doubleday.

Wigginton, E. (1975). *The foxfire experience.* Rabun Gap, GA: Foxfire Fund.

Yesseldyke, J. (1988, October 17). Keynote speech to the Special Service Education Department Second Annual conference on Assessment, Knoxville, TN.

Ziegahn, Learning, literacy, and participation: sorting out priorities. *Adult Education Quarterly, 1992, 43* (1), 30-50.

INDEX